WHITETAIL
THE ULTIMATE CHALLENGE

Text and Photography by
Charles J. Alsheimer

Published by

**krause
publications**

700 E. State Street • Iola, WI 54990-0001

Please call or write for our free catalog of outdoor publications. Our toll-free number to
place an order or obtain a free catalog is 800-258-0929 or please use our regular business
telephone 715-445-2214 for editorial comment and further information.

Library of Congress Catalog Number: 95-76857
ISBN: 0-87341-338-5
Printed in the United States of America

DEDICATION

To my dad, Charles H. Alsheimer, who planted

the seed for my love of hunting and nature.

And to the Lord Jesus Christ who has made

all this possible.

CONTENTS

ACKNOWLEDGMENTS

For over thirty years I've pursued whitetails across North America with gun, bow, and camera and this book is a culmination of these experiences. Along the way many people have helped me immensely; unfortunately space does not permit the mention of everyone who has made this book possible. However, there are a handful of people who have deeply touched my life and helped make this work a reality.

First, I'd like to thank Haas Hargrave and Dick Snavely. Both are outstanding businessmen and deer hunters who encouraged me to pursue a career in the outdoor field when others said it would be financially impossible. Their counsel birthed a dream that became a reality. Also, I would like to thank Larry C. Watkins, co-author of my first book, *A Guide To Adirondack Deer Hunting*. Larry got me started in the book-writing business and the learning experience we shared helped greatly with this one.

A special thanks is also in order to Jack Brauer and Al Hofacker, founders of *Deer And Deer Hunting* magazine. Jack and Al gave me my first real break in this business and coached and nurtured me through the early years. It is doubtful I'd be where I am today without them.

I'm also indebted to Debbie Knauer and the current *Deer And Deer Hunting* team and thank them for allowing me to reprint portions of my past DDH articles in this book. The relationship I've forged with DDH editor Pat Durkin over the years has been special. He's one of the finest editors a field editor can have.

To Outdoor Life's Gerry Bethge, Harris Publications', Lamar Underwood, and Northwoods Group's Lou Hoffman: I say thank you for your support and involvement over the years. You've made me a better writer and photographer.

To Erwin Bauer, Mike Biggs, and Lenny Rue ... America's "Big Three" in whitetail photography: Though they don't realize it, they have deeply inspired me to be the writer and photographer I am today.

To Paul Daniels, my neighbor, close friend, model, and in many ways the brother I never had, I say thanks for the memories. An outstanding whitetail hunter, Paul has gone out of his way to assist me in getting many photos, ones that would never have been possible without him.

To David Oathout, owner of Legend Lures: As friends we've spent hundreds of hours in the woods observing, photographing, and learning about whitetails and his insight into their behavior has helped me immensely.

My good friend and deer expert Ben Lingle, of Clearfield, Pennsylvania, has been an inspiration to me for years. He knows as much about whitetails as any man and has taught me a great deal.

This book could never have been done without the help of Bob and Alma Avery. Thank you for loving me, feeding me, "adopting" me into your family, and allowing me to photograph on your estate. Your mountain spread is truly heaven on earth.

George and Elizabeth Jambers of Whitsett, Texas, went out of their way to show me the "Real Texas." Their ranch and their love for this Yankee have touched me deeply.

A special thanks is in order to my country neighbor and friend Craig Dougherty, one of the sharpest minds in the hunting industry. Thanks for all your advice and insight.

But most importantly I want to thank Carla and Aaron. They're the greatest, most supportive family in the world. Carla is not only a wonderful wife but my best friend and my editor. And in spite of a career of her own, she is always there when I need her. And to Aaron...my son, my buddy, camera bearer, hunting companion, critic and model--all I can say is you're tops. Thanks for sharing North America's mountain tops, rivers, and forests with me.

FOREWORD

In my role as editor of *Deer & Deer Hunting* magazine, I always hesitate before opening photo and manuscript packages from Charlie Alsheimer. Why? Quite simply, I know the job ahead will be difficult. Every Alsheimer photo is exceptional, which makes it hard to decide which ones to keep and which ones to return.

At times I've asked myself what makes Alsheimer so exceptional in the highly competitive world of white-tailed deer writing and photography. Well, besides being an expert behind the camera and keyboard, he is even more serious behind a bow, shotgun or rifle. He hunts deer with passion and flexibility, always experimenting and adjusting his approach to take advantage of every changing situation.

And his interest in the whitetail knows no off-season. He laboriously manages his family farm in the oak-studded hills of western New York State for deer and other wildlife. In between planting a food plot or planning a logging cut, he's analyzing the habitat quality of his oak ridges and hemlock hillsides. And when he's not doing that, he can be found scouting bedding areas on hands and knees, or monitoring feeding areas from afar with binoculars or spotting scopes.

In short, many people are excellent hunters, many are excellent writers or photographers, and many are astute students of the whitetail's habits and habitat. Few, however, can combine those specialties and bring them to sharp focus for other deer hunters to appreciate and learn from. In that regard, Charlie Alsheimer is in a class by himself.

Alsheimer also has a unique understanding of what's important to deer hunters. No one will ever accuse him of being detached from his readers. For about three months each year he presents deer hunting seminars throughout the Northeast, which put him face to face with hunters and their questions. This allows Alsheimer to stay focused on what's important to deer hunters, and to pursue information they find useful. Whether it's the latest tips on rattling and calling, or the finer points of using decoys or scents, Alsheimer is always experimenting with new and old methods to find out what works consistently.

In fact, perhaps Alsheimer's greatest strength is that he never forgets what deer hunting means to his readers. Nor does he forget that most of their hunting occurs close to home for deer that seldom will qualify for national recognition. He believes strongly that most of the best deer hunters in North America are the guys next door or down the street. Alsheimer, himself, fits that category. While his magazine work occasionally takes him to Canada, Texas or other famous regions, his favorite place to hunt remains his own farm. When autumn paints the oaks and maples with its red and yellow swatches, you'll find Alsheimer moving stands, cutting shooting lanes, and preparing scent posts to waylay deer that run his ridges. As a result, when you read his deer hunting insights, be assured that most of it was developed during his years of hunting and observing "home-grown" deer.

Finally, perhaps the No. 1 reason behind Alsheimer's success is his work ethic, which is reflected in how he hunts, writes and photographs. No one works harder or longer hours to perfect these crafts than him.

As you read this book, you'll benefit from Alsheimer's years of hard work, expertise and straight-forward approach to deer hunting. Never before has he shared so much of his deer hunting knowledge under "one roof." His is a book you can trust and count on to make you a better deer hunter.

Don't be surprised if you sometimes slow down while reading, and carefully soak in every detail on each page. Like many of Alsheimer's photos and magazine articles, you won't see or comprehend everything that's there until you look at it a second or third time. But if you're like me, you'll love such work.

Patrick Durkin
Editor, *Deer & Deer Hunting*

INTRODUCTION

I grew up with the white-tailed deer. Being raised on a rural western New York potato farm allowed me to form many opinions about this magnificent animal and from an early age I've studied and admired them. I'll never forget the time I saw my first trophy buck run across a plowed field on our farm. The image of hair and antlers floating across the ground was forever etched in my mind.

Now, after nearly forty years of pursuit, I'm happy to say that my love and respect for whitetails is greater than ever. I've been blessed to hunt nearly every game animal in North America with bow, gun, or camera and nothing stacks up to the white-tailed deer. It's simply the most beautiful and challenging big game animal on the continent. Nothing else is close.

As I write these lines it's Christmas eve. It has been a great fall, perhaps the greatest. Since New York's bow season opened on October 15th I've hunted whitetails from New York to Saskatchewan to Texas, forty-two days in all. On top of this there were thirty more days of intense whitetail photography.

Yes, the season was a blessing in so many ways. As I reflect back I can't help but thank God for what He's allowed me to do. He's given me the opportunity to live in the greatest country on the face of the earth and do something I truly love. I guess a man can't ask for anything more.

I realized a long time ago that life does not consist of possessions. It consists of relationships. And the relationship I have with whitetails is a special one. It's one of experiences, memories, and a lifetime of days spent in the woods. In the pages that follow I hope you will be able to draw from my experiences to not only make you a better hunter, but a better sportsman and observer of nature.

Charles Alsheimer
Bath, New York
December 24, 1994

chapter 1

ODOCOILEUS VIRGINIANUS

My earliest recollection of nature, when growing up on a potato farm in Western New York, was seeing a whitetail bound across the field next to our house. The beauty of its measured leaps made a lasting impression on me, and fueled my desire to pursue a career of hunting, writing about, and photographing these animals. For over thirty years I've pursued wildlife with gun, bow, and camera throughout North America and no animal captivates me quite like the whitetail.

In a sense America grew up with the whitetail as well. When the first settlers arrived on the eastern shores of North America, they found a paradise teeming with a variety of wildlife, with the white-tailed deer being the dominant big game species. Prior to the early settlers' arrival, the Indians had relied heavily on the whitetail for centuries as a source of food, clothing, and tools.

It's not known exactly how many whitetails inhabited North America when the Pilgrims landed at Plymouth Rock. Some have estimated that their populations were as high as 40 million, while others claim there were fewer than today's 19+ million. At any rate, the early whitetail numbers did not remain high for long.

After the Civil War, Americans became adventuresome. Many began moving westward, clearing the land for farming and industry. In the process both whitetail habitat and numbers decreased dramatically. With open seasons, no bag limits, and a demand for venison in the cities, market hunting became popular in many parts of the East. And by the late 1800s, whitetail numbers were fewer than 500,000 throughout North America--just a fraction of what they once were.

Around the turn of the century, a plea went out from sportsmen throughout America and game seasons were closed. Unfortunately the damage was done and it took decades for huntable whitetail populations to return to the eastern portion of America.

Biology

Today, the white-tailed deer numbers over 19 million and is the most plentiful big game animal in North America, with thirty recognized subspecies. These various subspecies range from as far north as the 52nd parallel in Canada to the equator in the south. The size of these subspecies varies greatly over their range. Generally the farther north one goes, the larger the whitetails are. For this reason, the Northern Woodland and Dakota subspecies are considered the largest.

In the northern reaches of the whitetail's range, a mature buck will be about forty-two inches tall at the shoulder, while in its southernmost region, a buck will be little more than half as

Due to open seasons, market hunting, and loss of habitat America's whitetail populations plummeted in the late 1800s. Thanks to sportsmen, this carnage ended and populations were restored to their original numbers. (Gene Hamman photo)

Varieties and Distribution of Deer

Ranges of Whitetail Subspecies

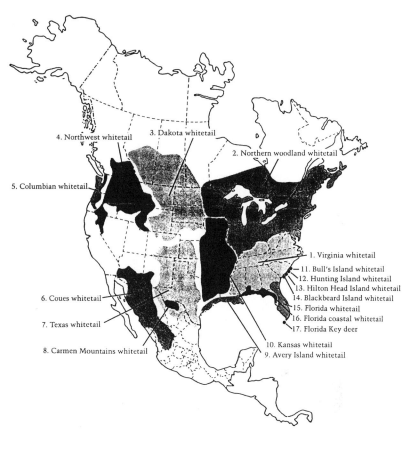

4. Northwest whitetail

3. Dakota whitetail

2. Northern woodland whitetail

5. Columbian whitetail

1. Virginia whitetail

11. Bull's Island whitetail
12. Hunting Island whitetail
13. Hilton Head Island whitetail
14. Blackbeard Island whitetail
15. Florida whitetail
16. Florida coastal whitetail
17. Florida Key deer

6. Coues whitetail

7. Texas whitetail

8. Carmen Mountains whitetail

10. Kansas whitetail
9. Avery Island whitetail

(Based on map by Smithsonian Institution)

tall. In many parts of North America, bucks that dress out over two hundred pounds cause a great deal of excitement. Though two hundred pounds seems to be a benchmark for big bucks, several dressing out at over three hundred pounds have been recorded.

In November of 1955, Horace Hinkley shot the heaviest buck ever officially recorded in Maine. The buck had a dressed weight of 355 pounds. It appears that the heaviest whitetail ever killed in the United States was taken by Minnesota hunter Carl Lenander, Jr., in 1926. It dressed out at 402 pounds and the state conservation department estimated the buck's live weight to be 511 pounds.

This mature whitetail scores 172 Boone and Crockett Typical, meeting the club's minimum score of 170 for Record Book entry.

What's a 140 Boone and Crockett typical buck look like? I own the sheds to this buck, which is shown here lip curling. It grossed an even 140 Boone and Crockett typical.

This velvet clad buck is considered a non-typical and would gross over 200 Boone and Crockett.

But perhaps the heaviest whitetail ever killed fell to archer John Annett of Ontario, Canada, in 1977. It dressed out at 431 pounds on government-certified scales. Unfortunately the buck was processed before Canadian authorities could examine it. Nonetheless, these weights show how big northern whitetails can be.

Though some states consider weight to be the key ingredient in determining how big a whitetail is, antlers are what make whitetails so popular. In the last two decades, more and more hunters have become knowledgeable about the Boone and Crockett scoring system and what it takes to grow a trophy buck. For over eighty years, Jim Jordan's ten point Wisconsin buck stood as the largest-racked whitetail ever killed, scoring 206-1/8 Boone and Crockett typical. Then in November of

1993, Milo Hanson of Bigger, Saskatchewan, killed a huge fourteen point buck that scores 213-1/8 typical.

It is generally accepted that a 140 class Boone and Crockett whitetail is a true trophy, wherever it is found. For a whitetail to be able to grow 140 inches of antlers, it usually needs to be at least 3-1/2 years old. Though a white-tailed buck may sport a trophy set of antlers at 3-1/2 years of age, it doesn't reach maturity until 5-1/2. And with the proper genetics and habitat, a 5-1/2-year-old buck can easily be in the 160-175 typical class.

With the huge interest in hunting mature white-tailed bucks, hunters are branching out across North America in search of a trophy animal. Rather than staying home to hunt the back forty, serious hunters are going to Texas, Kansas, Illinois, Ohio, Montana, and the western Canadian provinces in search of their trophy of a lifetime. (See Chapter 11 on Whitetails North And South.)

Spring and Summer

Spring is a time of birth and rebirth for all of nature. With spring green-up comes a dramatic change in the life of white-tailed deer. After a gestation period of approximately 202 days, the doe in the North gives birth around the end of May. From the age of 2-1/2 on, does may give birth to twins, if they are healthy and the winters are not severe. When twins are born, one will usually be a buck and one a doe.

Compared with other times of the year, summer is relatively uneventful for whitetails. During this time does are busy nursing and caring for their young, in preparation for the upcoming winter months. In June and July fawns grow by leaps and bounds and command center stage for those who love nature. I love to photograph fawns during the summer months, not only because of their beauty but because of their innocence. They are playful, therefore they exhibit some unusual behavior. Also, it is quite easy to call them within camera range, using a fawn or doe bleat.

With the arrival of the summer months, both bucks and does are busy gorging themselves on the preferred foods found in their home range. It's not uncommon for adult deer to consume between ten and twelve pounds of food each day.

Except in the most remote portions of their range, whitetails are grazers during the summer months, relying heavily on wild strawberries, alfalfa, clover, and other grasses. As summer blends into autumn, they begin browsing more frequently in preparation for winter. During the early autumn months beech-nuts, acorns, corn, and apples are among their favorite foods. When the frost has taken its toll on grasses and the fruit and

If conditions are right, does will give birth to twins in late May in the northern reaches of their territory.

mast crops are gone, whitetails turn to browsing. White cedar, apple, red and white oak, red maple, striped maple, staghorn sumac, witch hobble, and basswood are preferred browse in the North.

As the days of early spring become longer, a phenomenon known as photoperiodism causes a whitetail's antlers to grow. The increased amount of daylight activates the pineal gland that triggers growth hormones in a whitetail's body. It is this gland that determines when whitetails grow antlers, shed their antlers, change their seasonal fur coat, and breed.

In the northern region white-tailed bucks begin growing their antlers in early April. Growth is relatively slow throughout April and May; however, when the long days of June and July arrive, antler growth becomes significant. As the antlers grow, they are encased in a network of blood vessels and skin tissue called velvet, which nourishes the antlers throughout the growth process. By the end of August the buck's antlers are fully grown, have hardened down, and the velvet is ready to peel. During the summer months white-tailed bucks are secretive and move very

During the summer months velvet-clad bucks hang together in bachelor groups.

A buck begins to peel velvet at dawn.

little. They tend to bunch up and form bachelor groups and it's not uncommon to see four or five hanging together.

I've always been fascinated by the whitetail's annual antler cycle, from the time the bucks start to grow them in the spring until they cast them in winter. As a hunter and photographer, I've observed and photographed all stages of this cycle many times during the past fifteen years. However, one aspect of the antler process, the peeling of velvet, is something few have observed.

On August 31, 1989, while photographing on a large preserve, I was able to record this phenomenon on film. When I first located the buck at 7:00 a.m. in a swampy area, a small piece of velvet had already started peeling from one of the antler tines. From the time I started photographing, it took the buck fifty minutes to completely strip the velvet from his antlers.

During the fifty-minute period, I was amazed at the buck's behavior in attempting to strip his antlers clean. Throughout the process, he periodically licked all the blood off the alder

For the next fifty minutes the buck rubbed and thrashed his antlers against the brush to free his antlers of the velvet.

When all the velvet was peeled, the buck picked up the velvet and ate it whole.

bush he was rubbing before he peeled more of the velvet from his antlers. As more and more velvet began hanging from the antlers, the buck became violent in his attempts to remove the velvet. Several times the buck stopped, panted, and once staggered backwards, appearing to be exhausted. On two occasions he actually stopped and rested before continuing. After he freed all the velvet from his antlers, the buck scented the ground to locate the pieces that had been peeled off. Then, to my surprise, the buck picked up the velvet and ate it. I have since learned that bucks commonly eat their velvet, perhaps a behavioral trait to prevent predators from locating them.

One thing that sticks in my mind is the speed at which the buck removed the velvet and the violence involved in the velvet-shedding process. I've photographed several buck fights over the years and none was as violent as this buck's behavior. The annoyance of blood dripping and velvet hanging in its eyes probably contributed to this behavior.

Autumn

Though I'll elaborate more on the rut and whitetail behavior in later chapters, it's important to give a quick overview of autumn's happenings before going further into the text. By the time late September and early October arrive, the nights are cool and the year's crop of apples and mast start falling from

When autumn arrives whitetails gravitate to apples, making apple orchards prime locations to hunt.

the trees. Conditions are at their peak, and it's the grandest time of year for whitetails. In September, white-tailed bucks begin rubbing trees, and by October they start making scrapes throughout their territory. Bucks also begin sparring with each other to determine pecking order. The combination of rubs, scrapes, and sparring matches are preludes to the rut.

Autumn is also a time of chaos for the yearling bucks (1-1/2 years old). When October arrives, they usually break from their summer bachelor group and begin searching for their first home. At the same time they experience the first sex drive of their life. In many cases this hormonal infusion causes them to travel great distances. As a result, their process of looking for a new home range and dealing with their first mating season makes them vulnerable. Because of this, they are by far the easiest whitetail to hunt.

Some of the older does will come into estrus (the time when does are able to be bred) in mid-October, creating what is known as a false rut, which causes bucks to go into a frenzy. From this point until mid-November, when most does come into estrus, bucks become very active as they search for receptive does. In the process they rub, scrape, and fight. Though the peak of the rut varies throughout the United States, the activity associated with it is the same whether one hunts Texas, New York, or Alberta.

Winter

It's not uncommon for white-tailed bucks to lose up to 30 percent of their body weight during the rut. Therefore, once the rut is over bucks go into a feeding frenzy, trying to replace lost body fat before the harsh winter months arrive.

Winter throughout the whitetail range is incredibly varied. In the northern reaches January often brings harsh weather. For the next ninety days whitetails are subjected to ice, freezing rain, and snow, where snow depths exceed three feet in some regions. Significant snow depth forces a situation called yarding as deer bunch up and gravitate toward traditional food sources and cover. Unfortunately most yards' food has long ago been depleted, making it impossible for whitetails to find their daily requirement of seven pounds of browse. In addition to starvation, northern whitetails must also cope with the constant possibility of predation. As a result they are susceptible to coyotes, wolves, and dogs during the winter months when their strength is at its lowest. In many areas of the North, predation is significant. Unlike the North, snow and cold is not a factor for whitetail winter survival in the southern areas of North America.

Throughout most of the range, white-tailed bucks cast or shed their antlers between December and March, before beginning the growing process again in April. When the end of March arrives whitetails are far from sleek looking, and throughout most of their range they look gaunt from the rigors of winter.

Predators such as wolves, coyotes, and domestic dogs can be a real threat to whitetails during certain times of the year.

In most areas white-tailed bucks shed their antlers during the winter months. Then, in April the growing process starts all over again.

Also, to compound their gaunt-looking condition, they begin to molt in preparation for spring's arrival. But in spite of all winter is able to throw at whitetails, the majority survive quite well and live to see another season. The fact that they are able to survive from the equator to North America's far northern forest is testimony to their strength and survivability.

chapter 2

SCOUTING

Scouting is to deer hunting what spring training is to major league baseball. If a major league team doesn't work on fundamentals, fine tune its game, and come up with a plan to maximize its strengths, its chances for success when the season opens aren't very good. This also holds true for whitetail hunting. If you don't know where the deer are and how they react in different situations, it doesn't matter how good you can rattle, what kind of gear you use, or how well you can shoot. For this reason, scouting is the most important aspect of successful whitetail hunting.

In its simplest form scouting boils down to finding densities of deer sign. However, finding sign is only part of the deer hunting equation. Part two of scouting requires knowing what all the sign means. To do this requires a carefully thought out scouting plan.

Office Work

In order to maximize my efforts and minimize the time required for scouting, I use three different maps of the area that I intend to hunt. They are plat, topographical (topo), and aerial maps. Though all are different, each shows needed information about the hunting location.

The county plat map (often called tax or assessment map) shows who owns the land and is used by county assessors for assessing property taxes. Of the three maps this is the least important in terms of finding deer sign, but can be the most important when it comes to gaining permission to hunt a partic-

Studying aerial photos and topographical maps can help to shorten the scouting process.

ular area because it tells you who owns the land. Plat maps allow you to size up intended hunting grounds, as they show property boundaries, rivers, streams, roads, and buildings.

Topo maps are the second type of map I use for scouting. At first glance, topo maps seem rather complicated but they are easily understood after studying them for a while. The map's contour lines are drawn in such a way to allow cartographers to portray land elevations in feet (maps will tell you how many feet between lines, i.e., in flat country it's usually 5 feet, in hilly country 20 feet). The various lines allow you to identify the physical features of the land such as ridges, valleys, and benches on a side hill. Topo maps also outline in light green where the forests and woods are located. In addition roads and streams, and sometimes buildings, are shown on topo maps. In many parts of the country, topo maps can be purchased in local sporting goods stores. If this isn't possible, they can be purchased by contacting U.S. Geological Survey, Box 25286, Federal Center Building #41, Denver, CO 80225, phone (303)236-7477.

Aerial photos are the third type of map I utilize in the scouting process. Of the three maps I use this one the most, with the topo map being a close second. Aerial photos, or maps, come in two styles. One is a typical black and white photo. These photos

Aerial photos and topographical maps can reveal bedding areas, natural funnels, and feeding areas.

are to scale and can be purchased in a range of sizes from 10x10-inches to 38x38-inches. The other type of aerial photo is three-dimensional and requires 3-D glasses, called stereo-scopes, to read it. The three-dimensional photos appear blurred without the stereoscope, but with it the terrain's 3-D features jump out at you for careful scrutiny. The most popular three-dimensional size is 10x10-inches.

I use aerial photos produced by the U.S. Department of Agri-culture (usually taken every ten years). These can be purchased from any Consolidated Farm Service Agency office in the county you intend to hunt. Stereoscopes for use on the three-dimen-sional photo can be purchased from Monsen Engineering Com-pany, 960 South Main Street, Salt Lake City, UT 84101, or by calling (801)531-6505.

The aerial photos allow you to evaluate not only the area you intend to hunt but also the surrounding region. The photos encompass a lot of territory and show farm fields, wood lots, forests, ravines, streams, and roads, and enable you to get a feel for how a buck may be using a particular area. This is important because whitetails cover more ground than most peo-ple think. Research shows that a white-tailed buck's range includes anywhere from 600 to 3,000 acres. So it's important to have the big picture and aerial photos provide it.

Whitetail 101 states that whitetails need food, water, and cover to survive. The beauty of aerial photos is that they reveal possible food sources, funnels, travel corridors, and bedding areas. With a little practice you'll be able to pick out food sources and bedding areas on the photo, even to the point of being able to tell which trees are mature and immature; the mature trees show up as large dots and the immature ones as small dots. Generally dark dense areas on the maps with small dots signify dense cover, prime spots to be looked at as bedding areas.

By studying the three maps side by side, you'll be able to get a good overview and reduce the amount of fieldwork required to scout thoroughly. Also, by putting the aerial photos under plas-tic or glass, you can mark on the photo with a grease pencil where specific sign is located.

Actual Scouting

After studying the topo and aerial photos, the actual field scouting begins. As mentioned in the opening of this chapter, I'm looking for densities of sign. I'm a year-round scouter but my serious scouting is done between the months of December and May. One of the reasons for this is to keep from disturbing bucks too much in the fall. In addition to looking for shed ant-lers, another beauty of off-season scouting is that you don't

Finding old rubs in the off-season can reveal a lot about the size of bucks in the area.

have to worry about pushing deer into another hunter or forcing a buck into a nocturnal mode. You can't pressure mature white-tailed bucks and expect to see them during daylight hours. This is the biggest problem with fall scouting and is why I minimize scouting in the autumn. I'm convinced that if more hunters did the bulk of their scouting in the off-season, rather than in the fall, they'd have more success.

They say you find a whitetail through his belly. So, when scouting in the winter months I look for the whitetail's food source, both past and present. By December and January the fruit and mast is usually gone, but I scout orchards and oak stands anyway to see what kind of sign was left behind. If apples and mast were abundant in the fall, there should be lots of old tracks and droppings that would indicate how heavily the area was used during the fall. This allows me to know how the feeding areas might be used in the coming fall, if the food sources are similar.

Also, when scouting during the winter months I look for all the old rutting sign I can find, trails leading to and from the bedding and feeding areas, and how deer move through the area. When snow is on the ground I go into a possible bedding area and attempt to jump deer to see how they escape. Obvi-

A key to off-season scouting is locating a whitetail's bedding area.

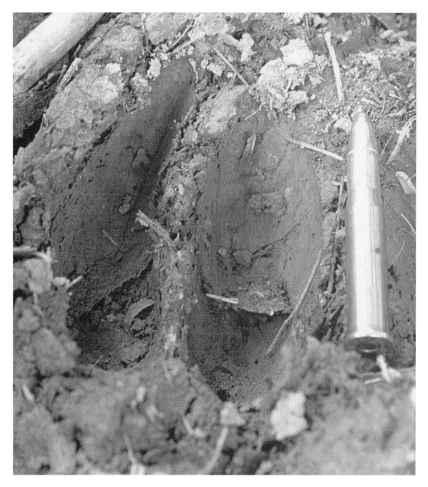

This track is over 2-1/4 inches wide and was probably made by a trophy buck.

ously, if you jump a lot of deer in midday, it's a prime bedding area. By finding escape routes I'm able to come up with a better hunting plan for the next season.

In addition, look for old beds in the bedding area. Often a buck likes to use the same bed over and over, if it gives him the protection he likes. When beds are found, sit in them and pan the area to see how well a deer can see from the location. Doing this allows you to see how secure deer think they are. If there are beds that show up in the snow, look to see if a buck has used them. Urine spots in the center of a bed indicate the sign was left by a buck. Urine on the edge of the bed usually indicates a doe. I always carry a small tape measure with me so I can measure the size of a deer's bed. Generally the bed of a doe

Prime scraping locations will generally show up in the same area year after year and can turn into prime hunting areas.

or yearling buck is 40 inches long, a 2-1/2-year-old buck's is 45 inches long, and a trophy buck's bed is 50 inches long. After checking the beds, look for the size of tracks left in the snow. If a track is over 2-1/4 inches wide, the animal probably weighs over 175 pounds and has trophy potential.

One of the best ways to learn about deer behavior during late season scouting is to follow them after you've jumped them from their beds. By using this technique I've learned a great deal about how bucks escape from hunters and travel through their areas. On other occasions I'll locate a known buck track and backtrack his trail to see how the buck moved through the woods and where he bedded.

While on the subject of deer movement, I look over the aerial photos and topo maps carefully to find the ridge lines, sags between two ridges, and benches on side hills. These are natural travel corridors and should be looked at closely when doing your legwork. In addition, I pay close attention to streams or rivers that intersect the property I wish to hunt, with the thought of locating key crossing points. Whitetails prefer to cross streams where the water is low and such crossing points can be excellent places to erect stands.

Though I'll go into scrapes and rubs in detail in Chapters 4 and 5, it's important to point out that I look in earnest for old rutting sign in the off-season because it can play a big part in my success the following season. I attempt to find old scrapes in or near bedding areas and along travel routes and funnels. It's important to realize that scrapes are signposts and often occur in the same places year after year, providing man or nature does not alter the landscape. So, knowing where these scraping areas are goes a long way toward preparing for the upcoming season.

Also, keep in mind that a mature white-tailed buck will often continue to work a prime scrape's licking branch throughout the year. As I mentioned, scrapes are signposts and just because the rut is over doesn't mean they will not leave their scent at a scrape. A way I tell if a buck is using a particular licking branch is to scuff out the earth under the branch. If a buck is using it, he'll leave his hoof print in the scrape for you to see. So, it pays to continually check for this type of sign.

Though scraping sign can be heavy in feeding areas, I don't take them seriously. Why? Because scrapes in feeding areas are seldom hit during daylight hours, especially after hunters invade the woods. By the time daylight arrives, bucks have already left the area to bed and in most cases when nightfall comes, bucks haven't reached the food source by the time a hunter must call it a day. For this reason, scrapes between the feeding and bedding area and in the bedding area get the bulk of my attention.

In addition to scrapes, look for big rubs in and around the corridors or funnel areas, along ridge lines, and around

This buck is working a signpost rub. These rubs are used year after year by many bucks and should be considered as a hunting location.

swamps. Though big bucks make both large and small rubs, big rubs will seldom be made by small bucks. So, the bigger the rub the bigger the buck. Like scrapes, rubs are signposts.

There's a lot of research being conducted relative to rubs, and one thing that's known is that the bulk of rubbing is done by mature animals rather than yearlings (bucks with their first set of antlers). In addition to single rubs, look for rub lines that will tip off a buck's travel route. Clusters of rubs will also reveal where bucks like to congregate. When looking at a rub, check it for any interesting characteristics that will reveal something different about the buck who worked it. How high are the gouges on the bark? If they are higher than normal and some higher branches are broken off, a mature buck was obviously working it over.

And lastly, don't rule out finding a true signpost rub. In areas where mature bucks are prevalent, finding signpost rubs can increase one's chances of hunting a slammer buck come fall. These traditional rubs are large and used year after year by resident bucks who seek them out as they travel their territory. Bucks not only rub their antlers on the signpost but also deposit scent from their forehead gland on the rub. This serves notice to every deer in the area of a buck's presence. Once, during a scouting session in February, I observed a big buck rubbing a signpost rub in spite of the fact he had no antlers. They had been dropped sometime previous to this encounter. Should you find a signpost rub, be sure to mark it on your aerial photo.

All the time I'm finding sign, I try to determine its relation to the cover, terrain, and feeding area. In other words I'm trying to find out how deer are utilizing the area. As I said in the opening of this chapter, finding sign is just the first step in the process; knowing how to analyze it is the second and most important part. When the feeding and bedding areas are known, the trails and escape routes are located, and the high-density sign areas noted, it's time to come up with a hunting plan for the upcoming season. The next few chapters will show how the sign can work to the hunter's advantage.

chapter 3

HUNTING BEFORE THE LEAVES FALL

There are four basic phases of whitetail hunting: pre-rut, chase phase, breeding phase, and post-rut. All are different and require different strategies. Historically, the whitetail's pre-rut has generated limited interest among deer hunters. Many view it as nothing more than a warm-up stage, a time to see what's in the woods, a time to start thinking about big bucks and the opportunities of November. Bow seasons open in September in many portions of the whitetail's range. In these areas, more and more hunters are realizing that whitetails often provide more, and better, opportunities before the leaves fall from the trees.

To better understand what the pre-rut (until about mid-October in the North) is all about, one should know a little about how whitetails live at this time of year. As a photographer and hunter I've spent thousands of hours during the last ten years observing, photographing, and hunting whitetails in every season and under every condition. These observations have given me some interesting insights.

As September eases into October the whitetail's thick winter coat grows in. This heavier coat, coupled with autumn's warm days, causes whitetails to be less active during daylight hours. As a result, they move at the edge of day and feed under the protection of nightfall. During this time a buck will seldom venture out of his core area, which is often little more than a square mile. On the other hand, does are biologically different and seem to continue their normal movement patterns. As a result, with doe sightings high and buck sightings low, hunting the pre-rut can be frustrating.

Research studies have repeatedly shown that bucks travel very little until about mid-October when their rutting switch is thrown. Three years ago the New York State Department of Environmental Conservation began radio collaring whitetails here in western New York to determine their movement patterns. Our farm is a part of the study area and it's been fascinating to see how these whitetails move throughout the year. Though the study has focused primarily on does, several bucks were collared as well. All the bucks move differently, but to date the study parallels the findings of previous research in that the bucks travel very little during the summer months, choosing to stay in a small area until mid-October when the rut starts. On several occasions I've traveled with the biologists to monitor the bucks and it's amazing how predictable they are in late summer and early fall. They are in the same general area day after day and all live where adequate cover, food, and water are in close proximity to each other.

During much of the pre-rut, bucks are still in bachelor groups. When mid-October arrives they will start to disperse and become much more aggressive toward one another.

Though bucks are secretive during this time, the added bonus of hunting pre-rut whitetails is that they are in bachelor groups and it's not uncommon to find several bucks together. I've had as many as seven bucks walk past my stand during an early season sit. But remember, once the rut starts to warm up, group behavior is over.

Around the end of August and early September, about the time bucks begin shedding their velvet, I start looking for rubs. These aren't the traditional rubs made by bucks when the rut approaches, but rather the rubs they create when peeling their velvet.

Food - The Key

As I mentioned in the last chapter, one of the keys to hunting whitetails is finding the food they like. Research shows that it's not uncommon for bucks to increase their body weight by 25 percent during the months of August, September, and October. The increased food intake occurs because once the rut begins, bucks do very little eating as the breeding urge overwhelms them. As a result they become determined and predictable in their quest for food during September and October. With this in mind, I begin scouting for available food sources in late July and early August. Due to where I live in the Northeast, I try to find locations where there is an abundance of acorns, beech-nuts, apples, corn, clover, and alfalfa.

Because of the whitetail's innate ability to determine which food is the most nutritious, I spend a great deal of time scouting for the best foods an area offers. Throughout the summer months I scout clover and alfalfa fields. Each of these foods has a protein value of about 20 percent and whitetails gravitate to them. Most of my hayfield scouting consists of the late evening variety done with the aid of binoculars or spotting scope. By keeping my distance from the wood's edge, I'm able to scout without pressuring the bucks. The type of cover around a hay-field is a key ingredient in determining whether a hayfield will be a candidate for early season bowhunting. Aerial photos can tell a great deal about this by revealing a wood's inside corners, where bucks often enter the field or natural funnels. On occa-sion I'll check the field's edge for the amount of droppings to determine how many deer are using the location. However, I try to keep this close-quarter scouting to a minimum so that I don't pressure the bucks I want to hunt when the season opens.

I also spend the warm days of August checking out the area's corn crop. During the late summer months, deer activity will not be high around cornfields, except early maturing sweet corn, but once October arrives and the field corn starts matur-ing, sightings will increase dramatically. As with hayfields, I'm

Acorn mast is a favorite of whitetails. Locating such mast crops will improve your chances come fall.

looking for cornfields that have attractive cover and natural funnels around them. Cornfields that have adequate cover can become real buck magnets throughout the fall, providing there is secure cover nearby.

Of all the food sources available to whitetails, none is as attractive as acorns. Acorns are nutritious and regardless of whether the acorns are white or red, deer abandon other foods in favor of them. The thing to remember is that acorns can be cyclical and just because there were acorns last year doesn't mean there will be acorns this year.

Last fall we had the best acorn crop in 20 years, but not the best autumn for deer sightings. Why? Because acorns were so abundant in our area, the deer were dispersed to the point they couldn't be patterned. From a hunting standpoint, the best case scenario takes place in years of marginal acorn mast. When this happens, deer will be concentrated and easier to figure out.

I begin scouting for acorns in earnest about the first of August. I've made it a practice to plot natural foods on my aerial photos in order to simplify scouting. To see if acorns are present I glass the oak canopy with a good pair of binoculars. In so doing, I'm able to determine what kind of an acorn crop there will be. Also, if the oak stands are located in a natural funnel area, the potential for deer sightings increases dramatically. In my area acorns begin falling near the end of August and bucks are quick to take advantage of the new supply of food. By checking for droppings, one can get a fair idea of how many deer are using the location and plan the fall's hunt accordingly.

Always remember that whitetails have a sweet tooth. As a result probably more pre-rut bucks have been killed in or near apple orchards than any other place. During the early autumn months, deer habitat is in a state of change and much plant life is stalky and not to a deer's liking. Consequently, when apples begin falling whitetails find them in a hurry. For this reason I pay close attention to apple orchards, especially old abandoned orchards that are choked with thick brush.

Hunting near cornfields can be especially productive during early bow season. The key is to find a buck's travel corridors in and out of the field.

The Setup

When scouting the pre-rut I look for well-worn trails near the food source. I also try to determine how far deer are traveling from their bedding area without actually going into them. The best time to do this is during late morning or midday when bucks are bedded. I do this because if deer have to travel very far to get from the bedding area to their food source, daytime sightings will be hard to come by. The key is to have your ambush point as close to the bedding area as possible, without being in the bedroom. This can be tricky and if you pressure bucks too much, especially mature bucks, they'll become nocturnal. And there is no harder buck to hunt than one that's a night owl. By setting up close to the bedding area you'll be able to intercept bucks as they head for the food sources at the end of the day.

If I'm hunting an apple orchard I scout for well-worn trails near the heaviest fruit bearing trees. Also, I begin looking for a good tree stand location when the apples start falling because bucks will be there to gorge themselves. If it appears that bucks are bedding close to the orchard, I'll attempt to erect a portable stand in the orchard if a given tree offers potential. However, if many trees in the area are bearing apples, my ambush strategy changes. Where multiple bearing trees are present, I locate my stand where the deer must pass to get to the orchard. Also, I place the stand at least fifteen feet high and no more than fifteen yards off the downwind side of the trail. If possible I also make every attempt to find a tree that will break up my outline because nothing is worse than looking like a lollipop in the sky.

I prefer intercepting bucks before they get to the apple trees because once they get into an orchard it is nearly impossible to determine which way they will go. Usually a whitetail will gravitate to whatever tree has the most apples under it on a given day. Normally there will be several trails leading into the orchard where a stand can be erected.

If the bedding area around a food source is not well defined, deer will come to feed from any direction. If this is the case I'll work the wind and erect the stand where I find the most sign, and move accordingly if needed. The sign I'm looking for is heavy mast on the ground and concentrations of droppings. These two things will give me an idea of how the area is being used.

When choosing early season stand locations, focus on areas where food, water, and cover are in close proximity to one another. Remember, in most areas a white-tailed buck travels very little in September and early October, so if your stand is in an area where the three necessities are met, your opportunities will increase.

Setting up along a well-used trail can be a productive way of intercepting deer as they move between their bedding and feeding areas.

When October arrives, bucks will begin to heavily rub as the rut approaches. Pay close attention to these rubs as they'll reveal how the area is being used.

Erecting tree stands along well-used trails leading to the field can provide a good deal of action when hunting near hay fields, cornfields, or grain fields. Also trails that meander toward bedding areas offer excellent opportunities for stand locations, especially where several trails merge.

Again, always make sure your stand is downwind of where you expect to hunt. If it isn't, move the stand. Nothing will destroy all your preseason scouting faster than not working the wind in your favor. There are many ways to fool a whitetail, but his nose is not one of them. Generally there will be more moisture in the air in the morning than the afternoon. As a result scent lingers longer in the morning. Also, I prefer a little breeze as opposed to none at all. Why? Because a small steady breeze will carry scent directly downwind and away from where you expect a buck to show up. If there is no wind, your scent will ride the thermals (drafts caused by the heating and cooling of the earth's surface) around your stand and cause potential problems.

The prospects of hunting can be challenging in hilly country, where terrain causes the wind direction to constantly change. However, if there is no wind, hilly country can be hunted very well if you remember a couple of things about thermals. In the morning as the ground warms, air will rise causing the thermals to blow uphill. In the afternoon as the ground cools, the wind reverses and blows downhill.

Over the last few years cover-up scents have become popular. By spraying a good cover-up on clothing and wiping a cloth laden with cover-up on the back of the neck and face, much human odor can be eliminated.

In the North I've always found the evening sit to be the most productive during the pre-rut, from a deer sighting standpoint. This has a lot to do with the fact that deer have been bedded all day in the warm temperatures and are eager to get feeding as the coolness of night approaches. And lastly, remember that the early season sign is temporary and things change rapidly as the food sources and sexual habits of bucks change. And when things start to change toward a rutting mode, you'll have to change your tactics accordingly.

chapter 4

THE RUT - WHEN BUCKS GO BONKERS

Behavior

The rut is the most popular time to hunt whitetails, period. Hunters can talk all they want to about pre-rut and post-rut hunting, but the rut, when bucks go bonkers, is the fuel that fires the deer hunting experience.

When mid-October arrives, the rutting switch is thrown inside a buck's body. The days are shorter, cooler, and a few does are starting to "smell right." All of this triggers the rub, scrape, and chase phase of the rut. This frenzy will last approximately thirty days and climax when the majority of the does come into estrus, which in most northern regions is from November 15 to 30.

What is this time like for a white-tailed buck? Let me illustrate. When September arrives the days are warm and the nights are cool. For the most part bucks hang in bachelor groups during September, bedding and grazing together. About this time, mast and apples begin falling from the trees, giving all deer a virtual buffet to feast on. This array of food is heavily eaten by both bucks and does during the cover of darkness. Bucks are also experiencing another phenomenon about this time, that of increased testosterone in their systems. This "natural sex drug" causes bucks to want to rub their antlers and spar with other bucks in their bachelor group.

As October arrives the testosterone valve is opened even more and bucks add a few more things to their daily routines. They begin scraping and "making eyes" at does around them. Also, their range begins to increase significantly over what it was in

When the rut begins bucks feverishly make rubs throughout their territory.

the summer months. During the rut it's common for a buck's range to encompass anywhere from 600 to 3,000 acres or more. When mid-October arrives a few of the older class does will come into estrus. The smell of hot does causes bucks to go into a frenzy, and the competition is keen for the right to breed the first does of the season. When this occurs the chase phase of the rut begins.

Around the end of October bucks are literally making a scrape wherever an adequate licking branch presents itself. This may seem hard to believe, but through the years I've observed over 500 bucks at scrapes and the tendency is for bucks to work nearly every overhanging branch they encounter. Because the majority of these scrapes are a result of an instinctive action brought on by a buck's sex drive, most scrapes will not be revisited. However, some of these scrapes, because of their location, will become prime scrapes or "bus stops" for bucks when November and the rut arrives.

In whitetail country November bursts onto the scene. Now the mornings are frosty and bucks are on the move. Around the first week of November it seems as though all bucks get another infusion of testosterone. With their latest fix, scraping, rubbing, and chasing replace eating. Sleep is hard to come by for bucks and aggression is at its highest. The entire deer family quickly realizes that a mature buck is nothing to mess with. A buck with several ruts under his belt not only chases every doe he encounters, but he also wants to kill the bachelor bucks he spent the summer with. The woods seem chaotic for most of the deer.

Finally mid-November arrives. The majority of does come into estrus and the breeding begins. If two mature bucks find themselves vying for the same doe, a fight to the death may ensue. If it does the fight's sound is incredible as antler bashing, grunting, moaning, and brush breaking fills the woods for hundreds of yards all around. The sounds attract any buck who wants a piece of the breeding action. Around November 20 the breeding becomes full blown and buck sightings decrease. With the

During late October bucks make scrapes throughout their territory in an attempt to leave their calling card to other deer.

estrous smell in the air, nearly every hot doe has a buck in her thicket. Because an estrous doe smells right for up to seventy-two hours, a buck will stay with her and possibly breed her several times during this period. With the does now in charge, the only buck movement to be found is when a doe decides to move about to feed or a buck has completed his job of procreation and moves on to the next encounter.

As November winds down, fewer does are in heat and bucks begin to move again, looking for receptive does. November's thirty days have taken a heavy toll on a buck's body. The scars of fighting can be death warrants and in some cases bucks lose between 25 and 30 percent of their body weight. The weight loss alone causes many bucks to teeter on the edge of survival, as they face the prospects of what winter has in store.

The Heat Of The Rut

The following sequence appeared in the November 1993 issue of *Deer And Deer Hunting* and illustrates the true essence of the rut. I've hunted whitetails for over twenty-five years in various parts of North America but only witnessed the entire breeding ritual six times. This and the chasing, rubbing, scraping, and posturing white-tailed bucks often go through as the breeding ritual unfolds is truly amazing. Once the rut explodes, hunting whitetails takes on a whole new perspective. For the most part scraping activity decreases when the majority of does come into estrus. Also, depending where a hunter finds himself, hunting can be very good or very poor. As you will see in this photo essay, the hot doe attracts a lot of attention when she reaches ovulation and greatly determines where bucks will be found.

For over six hours on a crisp fall day in 1990 I had a ringside seat for the breeding phenomenon. The best part was being able to record the event on film.

It's been my experience that when a white-tailed doe reaches estrus, she creates a minor traffic jam in the woods as bucks gravitate to her. She smells right and they all want to breed her. I began photographing this sequence shortly after spotting a big buck chasing a doe on the side of a heavily forested mountain. It was about an hour after sunrise and at the time I did not notice other deer in the area. But within an hour five different bucks showed up to join in the contest to see who would breed the doe. Needless to say the dominant buck went out of his way to make sure he would be the one.

Had the other bucks not been present, the big eleven point would have been able to breed her much sooner than he did. Unfortunately the persistence of the five intruders kept this from happening. Like spokes on a wheel, the five surrounded the doe as the big buck tried to work her. Whenever the doe

Above: Other bucks try to move in, but the 11 pointer quickly runs them off.
Below: An 11 point buck approaches a doe in estrus, but she is not ready to breed at this point. The doe runs, doing her best to avoid the buck's advances.

would come near one of the five bucks, the dominant buck would chase off the intruder. Often, just before chasing, the big eleven point would give off a low, drawn out grunt or wheeze. Then, while he was chasing off one buck, another would move in on the doe. On several occasions it almost appeared the five lesser bucks were teasing the big buck. The scene resembled a tag team match.

Another buck starts to come to the scene of the estrous doe. The 11 pointer boldly runs him off.

Other bucks are in the area, so the 11 pointer rubs a tree to show his aggression and dominance over them.

Often during the six hour episode the doe would stop and stand or bed for extended periods of time. Whenever this happened, the big buck would stand or bed a short distance from the doe. At times he would be alert, while at other times he appeared to be in a stupor. Periodically he showed aggressiveness toward his competitors by raking branches and working scrapes. In most cases throughout the morning he would do this within thirty yards of the doe. While the eleven point displayed his might, the doe and other bucks just stood and watched.

Though not the case here, I'm sure a fight would have ensued had any of the five bucks been equal to the dominant buck. Because all were smaller they were content to encircle the doe and let the bigger buck chase them off when they approached too closely.

Nearly three hours into the ritual another buck, a spike, attempted to join in. He obviously did not see the big buck standing in a thicket of hemlocks as he cautiously approached the bedded doe. While walking in on the doe, the spike gave off several low guttural grunts. All the time the eleven point was nearby watching. Through my lens I could see the big boy was

The buck approaches the doe's rear, and smells her rump to see if she is ready.

The 11 pointer, in one motion, mounts the doe and begins to breed her. He stays on her back about 15 to 20 seconds until the breeding is complete. During this time, the other bucks were off in the distance watching the event.

about to snap. When the spike got within twenty yards of the doe, the big buck wheezed and charged, nearly impaling the spike with his antlers. With all the commotion of leaves flying and branches breaking, the doe jumped up and ran off the mountain and into a swampy beaver flow.

The two largest intruders followed her off the mountain, appearing to go after the doe as a team. When the big buck saw what was happening, he left the spike and headed for the swamp. From my vantage point I was sure a fight would ensue, but it was not to be. After seeing what happened to the spike, both cowered at the eleven point's aggressive pursuit and ran off. Quickly the buck went looking for the doe in the swamp.

Quietly I made my way to the edge of the swamp. In a few minutes the doe emerged, stopped, and looked over her shoulder. Through my long lens I could see the buck appear. I could also see he was foaming from the mouth. He was pumped on hormones and ready to take on anyone or anything. In one last show of aggression he took out his frustration on a nearby tree. With his intruders gone he now had the doe to himself.

Nature had run its course. Rather than run from the buck, the doe was ready to stand and be bred. Slowly the big buck circled her and approached from the rear. After smelling the doe for a few seconds he began licking her flank. The licking went on for over a minute, then, in one motion the doe turned and he mounted and bred her. The breeding was over in thirty seconds.

This sequence, like others before, illustrated to me the difficulty of hunting when the rut becomes full blown. As shown here, six bucks gravitated to one doe. In doing so they left a void in another part of their territory. Many times throughout my hunting career I have hunted during the peak of the rut, in prime country, and seen no deer. There have also been many times when I seemed to be overrun with bucks. Two points to be made are that a hot doe is the ultimate lure, able to attract bucks from great distances. But most importantly, she controls the rut. And this point is the key to hunting as the rut unfolds.

Anatomy of The Rut

The two charts that follow illustrate the rubbing, scraping, and breeding dates for white-tailed deer throughout most of their range.

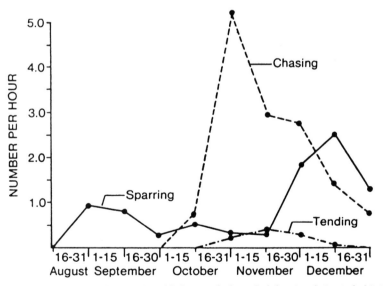

Hirth 1977 reference: Social behavior of whitetailed deer in relation to habitat. Wildl. Monogr. 53. Washington, D.C.; The Wildlife Society. 55 pp.

Sequence of sparring, chasing and tending acts by white-tailed deer at the Welder Wildlife Refuge in southern Texas.

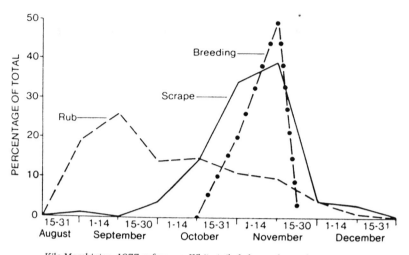

Kile-Marchinton 1977 reference: White-tailed deer rubs and scrapes; spatial, temporal and physical characteristics and social role. Amer. Midl. Natur. 97 (2); 257-266.

Frequency of rubbing, scraping and breeding activity by whitetail bucks during the rut.

Rubbing

When a whitetail's antlers reach their maximum growth in late summer, the velvet dries, cracks, and begins to peel. Therefore, locating rubs made by bucks peeling velvet is usually insignificant when planning your hunting strategy because of the randomness of where velvet is peeled. As the rut inches closer and closer to its November peak, white-tailed bucks increase their rubbing activity to both strengthen neck muscles and also to let other bucks know they are present.

In the process of making rubs, bucks leave their visual calling card. In addition to being dominant markers, rubs are also scent posts. When rubbing their antlers on the tree, bucks rub their forehead gland and nose on the rub, and will almost always lick the rub surface to leave their distinct odor. Though other bucks can visually relate the size of the rub to the size of the animal, it is the odor left on the rub by a buck's forehead gland that often lets other bucks know who's been there. It's been my experience that this, as much as the size of the rub, determines an adult buck's social status within a given territory. Also researchers believe that the pheromones bucks leave on rubs serve as a priming function that influences the timing of the rut (Atkeson & Marchinton 1982).

Throughout the rut bucks make rubs to strengthen their neck muscles and show their dominance. Locating a rub line can prove to be an excellent place to hunt.

Scraping

Of all the sign left by whitetails, scrapes get the most attention from hunters. Over the last fifteen years I've studied and photographed the whitetail's scraping behavior and with each passing year become more and more intrigued by this phenomenon. My opening commentary and the previous charts reveal when most scraping takes place. Like rubs, scrapes are signposts or sign markers that bucks leave throughout their territory to alert other deer of their presence. The beauty of this is that bucks establish a network of scrapes and regularly check them in their travels. It's important to note that some of these scrapes will become primary scrapes, and will be frequented more often by bucks as the rut progresses. Also, as the rut becomes full blown, does will work these scrapes as they come into estrus. So, an area where a prime scrape is located is the place to hunt (more on this later). Unfortunately, research has shown that nearly 70 percent of all scraping activity takes place under the cover of darkness. Even so, primary scrapes are often buck magnets, places where I do most of my hunting.

When a scrape is made, a buck is trying to leave as much of his scent (pheromones) as possible. In the process of making a scrape he rubs his preorbital and forehead gland, as well as salivating on the scrape's overhanging licking branch. He also paws away debris beneath the branch so he can urinate into the scrape's exposed earth. In the North a buck will usually splay his legs during the urination process, if the scrape is made prior to about October 25. After this time, he'll place his hind legs together and urinate through his tarsal glands into the scrape, while rubbing these glands together. By urinating through his tarsal glands, a buck is able to leave even more of his scent.

The following sequence shows how a scrape is made, from start to finish. It was photographed in the Northeast on October 20 as the rut was heating up. In the first photo the buck begins the scrape by working the licking branch, to leave as much of his scent as possible. Once done he immediately paws the ground to clear the leaves out of the scrape. The last step is to urinate into the scrape. Once November arrives the buck will put his hind legs together during the urination process.

When a buck begins to make a scrape he will work the overhanging licking branch, then paw out the ground, and conclude by urinating into the pawed out earth.

More than one buck will work a prime scrape. A few years ago while bowhunting over an active scrape on our farm, I had seven yearling bucks work the same scrape between dawn and 9 a.m. At one point one was working the scrape and another waiting his turn fifty yards away. Though I've never seen this repeated, I have photographed two big bucks working the same scrape within five minutes of each other. When I photographed the following sequence, I was sure the bigger buck was going to pick a fight with the lesser ten point. The small ten point (about 120 Boone & Crockett) approached the scrape and worked it in the usual manner. About the time he was finished, he turned and looked in the direction from which he had come. What he was looking at was a 160 class eleven point approaching the scrape. When the big buck got about five yards from the smaller buck (who was still standing in the scrape) he stopped, pulled his ears back in an aggressive fashion, and stared down the smaller buck. As the smaller buck left, the big buck began working the scrape.

More than one buck frequents a scrape at the same time. As in this case the smaller buck usually backs down and gives way to the bigger buck.

When the evenly matched bucks got within five yards of each other, it was apparent a rumble was about to commence.

The Fight For Dominance

An aspect of whitetail behavior that is seldom seen is the knock-down, drag-out fight, a fight that takes the participants to the edge of death. Over the years I've photographed and observed many sparring matches between white-tailed bucks. In the true sense sparring is not fighting, though it may appear as such. A sparring match between two white-tailed bucks is like a friendly wrestling match; the two participants merely push and shove each other around. Sometimes these sparring matches last up to a half hour or more, though most are reasonably brief.

Fighting on the other hand is a serious matter between two white-tailed bucks. When two equal size bucks find themselves on the range where competition is strong for the available doe population, fights to the death are a real possibility. One of the best fights I ever witnessed took place a few years ago in far south Texas. One morning, while photographing in a clearing frequented by both bucks and does, two equal size bucks appeared along with three does. When the bucks got within fifty yards of each other, they started posturing aggressively by pulling their ears back, standing their hair on end, and walking stiff-legged. For a couple of minutes they shadowed each other, in an attempt to bully each other out of the clearing.

Neither one would be bluffed, and when they got within five yards of one another, it was apparent a fight was about to com-

After a quick staredown, the bucks came together with tremendous force.

The fight only lasted about ten minutes, but I was sure one of the bucks would die before it was over.

mence. After a quick stare-down the two bucks came together with a tremendous force. The fight only lasted about ten minutes, but during this time I thought one of the bucks would surely die before it was over. The small clearing took on the appearance of a boxing ring as the bucks grappled over an area seventy-five yards in size. Dirt and dust flew in every direction and during the short time the fight took place, the bucks pushed, shoved, and threw each other around with ease, demonstrating their incredible strength.

Dirt and dust flew in every direction.

The bucks pushed, shoved, and threw each other around with ease, demonstrating their incredible strength.

Though I was positioned fifty yards from the fight, the sounds coming from the bucks were quite loud. In addition to the sounds of antlers coming together, both bucks grunted and bawled a great deal. Some of the grunts were short but many were drawn out. Then, as quickly as the fight began, it ended when the smaller eight point broke and ran for cover, with the bigger buck in hot pursuit.

I've seen fights like this throughout the whitetail's range and on each occasion have been in awe of the strength they exhibited. Unfortunately, fights of this nature are seldom seen.

The sounds of battle were quite loud.

Besides the crashing of antlers, both bucks were constantly grunting and wheezing. Some of the grunts were short but many were drawn out.

chapter 5

HUNTING THE RUT

After years of viewing rutting behavior from behind the lens of a camera and extensive hunting with bow and gun, I've come to realize the rut is the whitetail's shining moment. Because my career revolves around the whitetail, my biological clock, so to speak, is set for mid-October. It's the time I get serious about hunting with camera, bow, and gun.

Though white-tailed bucks scrape, rub, and chase does, it's the does that create the rut. Therefore, my hunting strategy revolves around pursuing mature white-tailed bucks, as they react and interact with the doe groups that frequent the area I hunt.

As already mentioned, a whitetail's rutting switch is thrown around October 15 (in the North). For the next thirty days he gets an ever-increasing case of "sexitis" until the breeding begins in earnest in mid-November. From the end of October until mid-November, whitetails are in what I call the chase phase or bonker stage. It's during this time that they let their guard down and are most vulnerable. Once the rut becomes full blown, a buck will become harder to hunt because of the does he's around. So the best window of opportunity for hunting rutting bucks is during the chase phase, specifically the last week in October until mid-November in the North.

A whitetail's range can be broken into three zones: feeding, bedding, and the area in between that I call the transition zone. If pressure isn't severe, the transition zone is where I ambush most of my rut bucks. Why? Five reasons: 1) Because mature bucks seldom frequent feeding areas during daylight hours. 2) If they do, there are usually does nearby and the scene can resemble a fire drill when the chasing starts. 3) With several deer in the feeding area, you have all kinds of eyes to contend

Big rubs in the transition zone are key tips to a big buck's location.

with before the moment of truth arrives. 4) You must stay out of the bedding area in order to keep a slammer buck from changing his habits. 5) The transition zone is where much of the rutting sign will be found and where a buck is most vulnerable. So, the majority of the time I hunt transition zones in an attempt to kill a mature buck. Generally a transition zone can be an area anywhere from fifty yards to over a mile in length; it all depends on how far the bedding area is from the feeding area. The key ingredient is that the transition zone offers secure cover in the way it connects the bedding and feeding area. If a transition zone is thick or happens to be a natural funnel, your chances for success increase.

If conditions and habitat are right, a number of trails pass through a transition zone. It's along and near these trails that I look for key rutting sign when mid-October arrives. As with pre-rut scouting, I go into the areas between mid-morning and noon and try to be as inconspicuous as possible while searching for sign. Generally I don't have to spend a lot of time in any one location because my off-season scouting has shown me where to look.

As the rut intensifies three types of scrapes will show up: boundary, secondary, and the primary. I pay little attention to boundary scrapes, except for checking the size of the track in them. As mentioned in the scouting section, the size of the track can determine if a mature buck is working the area. Boundary scrapes are random scrapes bucks make as they travel through their territory. They often show up along the edge of fields, fence rows, old roadways, and along creeks. So, as the name implies, they are along boundaries. Many boundary scrapes are made by yearling bucks as they try to figure out their first rut.

Secondary scrapes can offer excellent chances to kill bucks because they are generally found along well-used trails between the bedding and feeding area. In many instances bucks make a line of these scrapes (20 to 50 yards apart) along trails between the bedding and feeding areas. Because they are on trails, bucks will frequently rework and freshen them.

The "mother lode" of scrapes is the primary scrape. The primary scrape is the true "bus station" for white-tailed bucks and the one all hunters yearn to find. Unlike secondary scrapes that are placed on trails, primary scrapes are made in strategic locations and during the course of the rut, trails are made to them. They are often in thick cover where mature bucks feel secure.

Doctoring Scrapes

Basically I attempt to plan my scrape hunting near three different scraping locations, rotating among them so as not to over-hunt any one. A key thing I look for in determining these locations is cover. Because I'll be rattling and calling from these ambush points, I look for hot scrapes where there is medium to heavy cover (more on this later). Once I make a decision on a scrape location, I begin doctoring it. Not all scrapes are candidates for doctoring or using lures in the area near them. I've found that huntable scrapes need to be on flat or fairly flat ground in well-used whitetail travel corridors (funnels) that give bucks a sense of security. Though many hunters make mock scrapes, I do not. Rather, I find a natural scrape and proceed from there.

To make lures shine, find a primary scrape or secondary scrape to hunt over. The most critical aspect of scrape hunting is to make sure there is a good licking branch above the scrape. Remember, whitetails work the licking branch far more than pawing the ground, so the branch is the key part of the scrape.

Using lures to attract bucks was in part an outgrowth of my days as a fox trapper. Through experiences as a trapper I realized my chances of trapping a fox increased in direct proportion to the amount of fox scent I had around a set. Because of this I felt confident that deer could be lured within bow, gun, and

Two bowhunters put lure into a scrape during the doctoring process.

camera range in much the same way. By using the premise that a whitetail scrape can be made to resemble a fox set, at least in principle, I've been successful over the years at making certain scraping locations into whitetail magnets with the use of lures.

When I trapped fox I used to make the set hotter and hotter by applying liberal amounts of red fox urine around the bait and set. Also, if I caught a fox I'd try not to disturb the set because I knew the odor left by the fox would enhance the set, making it more attractive to other fox in the area. I'd also make a scent post near the set so a roving fox could smell the location from a distance. In all cases I made sure I left no human odors behind.

I share this fox trapping scenario because I use the same principle when using deer lures around scrapes and when making scent trails. I begin by making sure that I leave no human odor around the scrape I intend to doctor. I use 35mm film canisters with the top half perforated with holes and boil the canisters in water prior to use, to kill human odors. Inside the canister I place three cotton balls to ready them for hanging above the licking branch.

I also wear knee-high rubber boots when hunting around the doctored scrapes and going to and from the area I intend to hunt. In order to eliminate human scent on the boots, I periodically wash them with soap and warm water, then rinse them with boiling hot water. I also use latex gloves when tying the scent canisters above the scrape, to protect against leaving human scent behind. From an equipment standpoint, I often carry a small de-scented trowel to work the scrape's dirt under the licking branch. No doubt this sounds extreme but these are all precautions fox trappers take and I believe that if you can beat a red fox's nose, you can beat a whitetail's as well.

Since the late 1980s I've been using three deer lures to hunt whitetails. Two I'll discuss now and the third later. One I make with the vaginal discharge from Holstein dairy cows and pure whitetail urine. The other is a commercial lure, Horn Hunter Buck Lure (800-835-4310), which contains Holstein vaginal discharge, pure whitetail urine, interdigital gland, and tarsal

A buck works a scrape's licking branch to leave his scent.

Adding lure to the scent canister over the scrape is part of the doctoring process and makes the location more attractive.

gland. It's a great lure and has all the key ingredients required to attract a buck.

No doubt using the vaginal discharge from dairy cows comes as a shock to some. I began using the Holstein vaginal discharge lure in 1982 (I gave it the name white lightning) when I heard of a dairy farmer from a neighboring state who killed a record whitetail with bow and arrow. What was unique about this successful bow hunter was that he used the vaginal discharge from his dairy cows as buck lure. To be more exact, he collected only the discharge from cows in the peak of their estrous cycle.

In 1988 I first wrote about using white lightning in *Deer And Deer Hunting* magazine and since have been contacted by farmers, artificial inseminators, veterinarians, and lure companies who have concurred that other ruminant's vaginal discharge will work to attract whitetails. I also had communication with a popular lure company that uses the vaginal discharge from goats (another ruminant) in the manufacture of its deer lures. Needless to say the last few years have been an interesting learning experience.

A key aspect of using lures successfully is that they need to be fresh in order for them to work. Regardless of whose lure is used, freshness is essential because the pheromones in the lure dissipate rapidly. For this reason I refrigerate my lures, try to use them within two weeks of opening the bottle, and never carry the lure over to the next year. In addition to the lure's pheromone dissipation, it's important to use the vaginal dis-

The purpose of the scrape's scent canister is to lure bucks to the scrape.

charge lure before air begins turning it to ammonia while still in the bottle.

To doctor the scrape I tie one or two scent-laden canisters on the licking branch, at least six feet off the ground. Once done I fill the canister with homemade or commercial lure. I do this with an eye dropper, inserting the lure through a large hole in the side of the canister. This can be an expensive step as it takes about one ounce of lure to fill the 35mm film canister.

No doubt many will wonder why I use vaginal discharge lure above the scrape. After all does and bucks urinate on the ground, not in the tree branches, right? Well, I used to think this way but after a good deal of experimenting I've found that bucks don't seem to be concerned about where the smell is coming from. Having the canister in the air allows bucks to smell the lure from farther off.

Lastly, I do one rather radical thing at the scrape site during the doctoring process. Earlier I mentioned that I use three different lures. Well, the third one is my own urine. When I'm hunting over a particular scrape I'll urinate into it after my morning sit. The tactic will no doubt shock some but I've used it for nearly ten years and like many hunters find it to work well. However, if you are on medication don't use your own urine. In most cases the medication will foul the urine and spook any nearby deer.

Fox trapping taught me that I was more successful when I could make a set as powerful smelling as possible. So, by urinating into a scrape I'm able to put over ten ounces of "lure" into the scrape's fresh earth. If I were to place a commercial lure in the scrape's dirt it would cost roughly $75 ($7 per ounce) every time I doctor a scrape. However, this isn't the only reason I do it. I do it because it works.

Both human and whitetail urine are animal urine by nature and they both give off the same ammonia smell after being exposed to dirt and air. Because of this I urinate into scrapes to make them more powerful smelling. I've doctored scrapes in this fashion from Texas to Saskatchewan to New York and never once have I seen a buck become alarmed. In all cases they smelled the ground and worked the scrape before moving on. It's a way of making a scrape hotter without killing one's pocketbook.

It's important to point out that I never use human urine to doctor scrapes at the end of the day. Whitetails are on the prowl at dusk and I don't want to risk spooking them before the urine breaks down. Also, I never use human urine in scent canisters as they're only for the vaginal discharge lures.

To keep the scrapes as hot as possible I replenish the lure in the canisters every other day. The important thing is to keep the odor strong. Also, fresh earth under the scrape seems to be an attractant, so I make sure that the scrape beneath the licking branch is kept roughed up and free of debris.

This buck has smelled a doe's urine and is lip curling. This allows him to determine if she is in estrus and ready to breed.

Making The Scent Trail

Another way I use lures is by making scent trails in and out of the woods I'm hunting. This great tactic is one used by deer hunters across America. There are any number of ways to lay a good scent trail. Some hunters drag a scent-laden rag behind them as they walk into the woods while others use scent pads on the bottom of their boots. Personally I periodically squirt my

This farm country buck is proof that scent trails work. Two hours after laying a scent trail he walked right to my stand.

estrous lure on the bottom of my rubber boots as I walk into my stand, starting the process when I'm within 100-150 yards of where I intend to hunt. I walk past the stand, making the trail where I would like a buck to follow, then backtrack and get into the stand.

I killed the buck in the previous photo in 1989 using the above described scent trail technique. It was November 3 and I laid a scent trail on my way into the stand, which was near an active scrape. I climbed into the stand around 2 p.m. and waited about an hour before going through my first antler rattling sequence of the afternoon. I got no response. Around 4 p.m. I decided to rattle again. Just as I stood up to take the antlers off a limb, I looked to my right and saw this buck coming down my scent trail, nose to the ground with his tail outstretched. When he got about twenty yards from me, he paused and I put an arrow right behind his front shoulders. I've had similar examples of this down through the years and it illustrates how successful scent trails can be.

The Stand Location

Setting up the ambush over a primary or secondary scrape can be tricky. First, try to find a hot scrape as close to the bedding area as possible. By doing so you'll be in a better position to intercept a buck visiting his scrape during daylight hours. Remember nearly 70 percent of scraping is done under the cover of darkness, so by being as close to the bedding area as possible you can intercept a mature buck when he leaves his bedroom at the end of the day. If you set up too far from a bedding area, the buck won't reach you before quitting time. The same holds true in the morning, though it is not as critical because during the chase phase of the rut (early November) bucks are on the prowl until midday. But by being close to the bedding area you can catch a buck returning to his bedroom.

Stand placement in relation to the scrape is critical when bowhunting. Often terrain will dictate where this will be. If possible I set up 25-60 yards downwind of the scrape rather than right on top of it. I used to set up within 15 yards, but consistently found mature bucks going downwind of me as they passed through the area, scent checking the scrape. In a few situations these lessons were learned the hard way. By moving farther from the scrape, and laying a scent trail, my opportunities to kill mature bucks increased. Of course gun hunting over scrapes is a whole different ballgame and doesn't require the detailed preparation because distance isn't a factor.

As I mentioned before, I like to hang a stand in fairly thick cover so I can incorporate calling techniques into the scraping process. When rattling you need to obstruct a buck's view when

The perfect setup. A buck working a doctored scrape with a bowhunter ready to shoot.

he comes looking for the two combatants. Because I'm usually set up in thick cover I don't go over fifteen feet high with my stands. If you go higher the forest's canopy causes problems with tree branches, etc., being in your way. The downside of setting up in thick cover is that at times I will not be able to see my doctored scrape. However, I don't view this as a major problem because of how I incorporate my scent line, rattling antlers, and grunt tube into the hunt. When bowhunting near scrapes in close quarters, I seldom sit when on stand because I've learned deer can surprise you at any time. The moment of truth can be a bang-bang affair and by standing, at ready, you're better prepared for the magic moment.

Rubs and Rub Lines

Often where you find scraping you'll find rubbing as well. They go hand in hand and when you find heavy rubbing in an area of heavy scraping your chances of success increase greatly. I always look for traditional signpost rubs wherever I hunt. Unfortunately it takes a good population of mature bucks for a true traditional signpost to exist. Therefore, throughout much of the whitetail's range, where 80 percent of the buck kill is yearlings, there are no signpost rubs. However, if one is found it's a real hotspot and a prime hunting location.

If a signpost rub cannot be found, look for big rubs, rub lines, and clusters of rubs in the transition zone. Rub lines often reveal the way a buck was traveling. If the scarred side of the tree faces the feeding area, the rub was probably made in the morning as the buck returned to his bedding area. If the scars face the bedding area, the rubs were undoubtedly made when the buck exited the bedroom in the evening.

As mentioned in the last paragraph, rubs can reveal how a buck travels and should get your attention. If there is a definite line of big rubs in an area, a stand should be hung downwind of it and that area hunted. These rubs were placed not only to let other bucks know who's boss but also to mark a buck's travel corridor.

If I'm bowhunting I set up about fifteen yards downwind from the rub line, in a tree that breaks up my outline. As with scrape hunting I seldom go higher than 15 feet. I hunt close to a rub line even if there are scrapes present because I know that the buck who made the line will travel it, rather than scent checking the scrapes in the area.

One piece of rubbing sign that really gets my attention in a scraping area is clusters of rubs. You might say they could be viewed the same way bulletin boards are at a grocery store. You know, a place where people leave their calling cards and notices of community functions. Not everyone reads them but bargain

An active signpost rub is a tip-off that big bucks are in the area. Note the big buck in the background.

hunters sure do. I view rub clusters the same way many view those grocery store bulletin boards--as bargains. Because when you find clusters of rubs in a prime scraping area you know there are a lot of bucks in the area. And if there is a good population of does, it's reason to be even more excited. In part this is because heavy rubbing by bucks leaves behind pheromones that induce does to come into heat. And with doe groups in the area, the chances of killing a buck increase dramatically as the rut progresses through the chase phase before climaxing in the breeding phase.

chapter 6

CALLING & RATTLING WHITETAILS

Whitetails are no different from other animals, in that they are curious creatures. Throughout their lives they communicate with each other using a variety of bleats, grunts, and snorts. For the first six months of life fawns bleat to their mothers. Adult bucks and does also communicate with each other by grunting. And, of course, whitetails use the snort to alert other deer of danger. During the rut, bucks also respond to the sound of two bucks fighting. As a result, using antlers, grunt tubes, and other calls to communicate with whitetails during the rut can be challenging, exciting, and on occasion, very productive.

When I first began using communication with deer I did so with only antlers. Though there were successes, it wasn't until I began using a grunt tube, alone and in conjunction with the antlers, that my success at luring deer close increased significantly. During the last ten years I've discovered that using a call will cause deer to be more responsive than anything else. For this reason my grunt tube goes with me whether I'm hunting with a bow, gun, or camera. Regardless of where I hunt in North America, I find that for every buck I rattle in, ten to fifteen will come to grunting and bleating.

Whether a novice or seasoned veteran, it's important to realize that you don't need to know how to make every vocalization a whitetail makes. I'm amazed at the number of different sounds seminar speakers tell their audiences whitetails make. After thirty years of hunting and photographing whitetails up close, I treat much of this entertainment jargon as suspect. As a seminar speaker I urge hunters to keep calling simple, by mastering two or three different sounds. By sticking to the grunt, doe

Next to the weapon you use, a grunt tube is the most important piece of equipment you can carry into the woods because of the way it can bring deer to you.

bleat, and on rare occasion the fawn bleat (a distress call), a hunter can cover all the bases in pursuit of white-tailed bucks.

For the most part white-tailed bucks make two kinds of grunts, contented and rutting. The contented grunts are brief and calm and made by both bucks and does to keep track of each other. Rutting grunts can be frequent, drawn out, and sometimes loud, especially when made by bucks in pursuit of an estrous doe.

When using a grunt tube to simulate a buck's guttural grunt, I advise hunters to call softly at first. It's been my experience that this is the most critical aspect of grunting for whitetails. Deer are vocal creatures, but most of their grunting is not loud. The only time I blow loudly on a grunt tube is when I've called a buck and he gives no indication of hearing me.

Deer calls are easy to use. Very little practice is required and by listening to a skilled caller, a novice can go into the woods and make realistic deer sounds. The key is to know when to use a specific call, be it grunt or bleat.

The sound of low guttural grunts will often lure more than one buck into range.

My 1991 New York shotgun buck provides an example of how I've successfully used a grunt tube. Thanksgiving day, 1991, was not a great day from a weather standpoint. It dawned warm, damp, and windless. In spite of the conditions, I headed for my favorite hemlock tree stand hoping for the best. Trying not to spook any deer, I slowly picked my way to the tree, which was located in the thickest part of a bedding area. I covered the five hundred yards to the tree flawlessly, but in the predawn darkness spooked a deer when I was halfway up the tree.

Not knowing what it was, I readied myself for a long sit. About a half hour after legal light, I heard a lone guttural grunt in the gully below me. I couldn't see a thing through the thick undergrowth but I knew a buck was someplace below. I brought my grunt tube to my lips and softly grunted twice. Within a minute I could see the wide-racked buck coming toward me, stiff-legged with hair on end and ears pulled back. In one motion I brought my shotgun up, put the cross hairs on his shoulder and fired. The big eight pointer never knew what hit him. Without the grunt tube I never would have had a chance at him.

It used to be that I would never use a deer call unless I saw a deer first. This is no longer the case. Often when still hunting I'll come across a location that looks right for deer. When this happens I'll find a spot that gives me good cover, get ready, then give off two to four short grunts or doe bleats. If there is no response I'll wait a few minutes before calling again. If I'm using the buck grunt, I'll often give off two or three drawn out grunts during the second sequence, which sound like a buck's aggressive grunt, to try and get a buck to respond. On several occasions during the last two years, this technique has offered opportunities to take bucks as they came to the sound of the grunting and doe bleating.

It's an excellent time to use a grunt tube when tree stand hunting and a buck walks through the woods out of range. When this takes place I'll begin by grunting softly on the tube to try and get the buck to stop. If he doesn't stop I'll grunt louder. Once stopped the buck will invariably look around to locate the sound. Then I'll grunt again, just loud enough for him to hear the grunt. If he begins walking toward me I don't grunt again unless he hangs up or changes direction. Using this technique can often put a buck within fifteen yards of your location.

The doe bleat is not as effective as the buck grunt but I've had a lot of success with it over the years. This call works well during the rut and I like to use it most when I'm on stand and the action is slow. Usually I will give out a series of three doe bleats, then wait about half an hour to repeat the sequence. If a buck is within earshot and interested, the sound of my doe bleat will often cause him to come looking. I view it as a real buck attractant during the rut when bucks are looking for any available doe they can find. I'll also use this call when hunting over a decoy if I need to get a buck's attention.

During bow season bucks will often come within fifteen yards of a stand as they look for the source of the grunting.

The fawn bleat is a distress call and I seldom use it during hunting season because it indicates stress and danger. However, I use it extensively when photographing does and fawns during the summer months. There is no better way to get a doe's or fawn's attention. I've lost count of the times I've called fawns within fifteen yards using this call.

Selecting a good grunt tube is not that easy. For the most part tubes are sold in plastic packaging, making it impossible to try them in advance. As a result, hunters often buy a tube not knowing what it sounds like. There are many excellent tubes on the market, as well as many poor ones, so it is vital that one knows what a given brand sounds like before buying it. It's also important that the tube require little effort to blow on it. Hunting in cold weather does strange things to a hunter's lips. If a tube requires a lot of effort to blow, the results can be discouraging. So, a word to the wise is if a tube takes more effort to blow than it takes to fog a windowpane, don't buy it. From a practicality standpoint, I use an adjustable tube that allows me to make both the doe bleat and buck grunts with one call. And lastly, make sure a given brand of tube can be blown loudly and still sound realistic. Many brands on the market sound like duck calls when a lot of volume is required.

Though I've found calling whitetails to be more successful than rattling, no aspect of deer hunting is more challenging than rattling in a buck. Once you have done it, you'll be hooked for life. During the last six years, while hunting in various parts of North America, I've rattled in over one hundred bucks.

It has been my experience that the prime time to rattle whitetails is during the two week period prior to the peak of the rut. Also, if the buck to doe ratio is no more than three to four does for every antlered buck, rattling will seldom work. The lower the ratio, the better the response because of greater competition for breedable does.

When rattling, I do it in a sequence involving three steps. Because few fights I've seen lasted more than five minutes, I rattle for about a minute and a half, pause for about thirty seconds, rattle for a minute and half, pause for thirty seconds, and conclude the sequence by rattling for another minute and a half. When finished I quietly lay the antlers on the ground or hang them up. During the sequence I also incorporate a series of grunts to add realism to the process. When bucks fight there is a lot of grunting and on occasion bawling emanates from the fray.

I begin the sequence by merely tickling the tines together for several seconds, then really get into it by rattling loudly and aggressively--the louder the better. I rattle loudly and aggressively because the best fights I've witnessed were noisy. Starting the rattling sequence with the tine tickling results from my desire to set up in thick cover. Because of this setup I start

During the two weeks prior to the peak of the rut bucks are often responsive to antler rattling.

softly, so as not to spook any nearby deer before my rattling gets louder.

Personally I prefer a natural set of 120-130 class antlers for rattling. The key is that they not be weather checked, otherwise they will sound punky. Soaking them for about two hours each year in a bucket of water will keep their tone accurate. Though I prefer natural antlers I've rattled bucks in with synthetic antlers. My major gripe with synthetics is that they are not heavy enough to project the amount of sound I want. In 1993 I took my rattling in another direction by rattling in and killing a 160+ gross whitetail in Saskatchewan with a Lohman rattle box. So, the key is not necessarily what you use to rattle, but what it sounds like.

Though I've killed bucks while rattling from both the ground and tree stands, rattling from the ground where I can make more natural sounds, like breaking branches and rustling leaves, has been more successful. Unfortunately, it is more difficult to get a shot from ground level, particularly with a bow, unless someone else is doing the rattling. Consequently, teaming up with another hunter can be a successful way to get a buck close.

When using the team concept I like to have a person rattling close to the shooter, and no more than twenty-five yards away.

Left and Above: Aggressive rattling will work better with larger bucks. These two photos show the aftermath of an aggressive buck fight. This buck was so exhausted that it didn't move for a half hour.

The most effective way to rattle during bow season is on the ground with the hunter in the stand.

The reason for this is that bucks will often circle the rattling sound, trying to get downwind. If the rattler is too far from the shooter, seldom does a shot present itself.

A common happening when rattling is to have a buck stop just out of range. Actually all he is doing is being cautious and trying to figure out where the fight is. When this happens rely on the grunt tube to bring the buck in close. Usually one or two soft grunts will coax him close enough for a shot. As mentioned previously, the key is to blow on the tube as softly as possible while still making sure he hears the grunt.

Generally the first and last two hours of the day are the best times to rattle. However, don't rule out midday. If there is a full moon during early November, rattling during lunchtime can be productive. Also, cool, overcast, windless days during early November are best.

When calling during the post-rut I use the grunt tube the same way as during the rut. However, if I use rattling antlers at all, I use them sparingly. Instead of rattling in loud sequences, I just tickle them together to simulate sparring bucks.

This buck is proof that rattling will work for big bucks. I rattled in and killed this one in Texas.

chapter 7

NOCTURNAL WHITETAILS

Nocturnal whitetails are the hardest to hunt. There are none harder. I've always been interested in the nocturnal aspects of whitetails, but during the last several years my curiosity has increased. Since 1988 I've seriously studied the nocturnal side of whitetails in an attempt to learn how to hunt them better and predict their movements. Research and personal observations have shown that two factors contribute heavily to whitetails becoming nocturnal creatures. First, the presence of human activity causes them to go "underground." Secondly, as a white-tailed buck grows older (over two years old), it has a tendency to become less and less adventurous, meaning he stays home and moves more and more under the cover of darkness.

After thousands of hours of nature photography and through combat experience in Vietnam, I've learned a few things about how animals adapt to danger. And this adaptation seems to be similar in all animals whether it's birds, deer, or people that are being studied. The following illustrates what I mean.

In Vietnam the Viet Cong loved to attack in the early morning hours, under the cover of darkness. As a result I was always on edge and more attuned to what might take place, especially when I had guard duty. Though I never got used to it, I did become a survivor. Vietnam taught me that you learn fast, if you can make it through the first encounter. Unfortunately many GIs didn't get a second chance, but those that did quickly learned survival skills.

This illustration says much about how whitetails adapt to humans. Always remember that a whitetail, buck or doe, is the ultimate survival machine. If a buck can survive his first season of encounters with man, he becomes a better survivor with each passing day. So, when the human element is introduced to the forests of America, the daytime patterns of all animals change. As a result, in areas of heavy hunting pressure, innovative tactics are often required to consistently kill bucks.

BEHAVIOR

In order to formulate a hunting strategy for nocturnal bucks, it's important to understand that all white-tailed bucks are not the same. They fall into two categories, yearlings and adults. This is especially evident in areas where hunting pressure is heavy.

Yearling bucks are much easier to hunt and it takes a lot of pressure for them to become truly nocturnal. As mentioned in Chapter 1, the sex urge of a yearling's first breeding season overwhelms most of them, keeping them constantly on the move. This makes them easy to hunt. However, if a buck is lucky enough to survive his yearling season, he becomes a totally different animal the second season, when he is two-and-one-half years old.

The two-and-one-half year old and older bucks are the ones that give hunters fits. They are also the ones that carry trophy antlers. Just how hard are they to kill? Let me illustrate. As

Mature bucks are totally different than yearlings. They are elusive and are easily turned into nocturnal creatures once the hunting season begins.

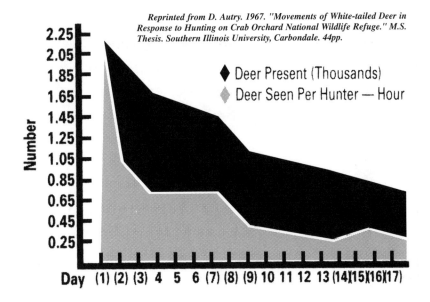

Reprinted from D. Autry. 1967. "Movements of White-tailed Deer in Response to Hunting on Crab Orchard National Wildlife Refuge." M.S. Thesis. Southern Illinois University, Carbondale. 44pp.

◆ Deer Present (Thousands)
◇ Deer Seen Per Hunter — Hour

This graph illustrates how hunting pressure affects deer sightings. With hunters in the woods deer move less during the daylight hours.

mentioned earlier, for the past three years the New York State Department of Environmental Conservation, under the guidance of Senior Wildlife Biologist Jim Fodge, has been studying radio collared whitetails in the area I live. There are three adult bucks in the study that are surviving quite well, in spite of heavy hunting pressure during gun season.

As a matter of fact, one of the collared bucks has not been seen by any of the landowners or hunters since it was a yearling. When he was a five point yearling I passed him up while bowhunting, as did another hunter. He's now three years old and no one knows what kind of antlers he has.

In March of 1994 I asked Fodge if it would be possible for us to try and get a look at the buck. On March 14, he and I and three other state wildlife personnel surrounded the woods where the buck was in an attempt to see him. Frankly I felt this would be easy because the buck's collar would show up well on snow, we had two radio transmitters to pick up his signal, and we were all seasoned deer hunters. I closely followed a technician who carried one of the radios and antenna, while Fodge entered the opposite side of the woods with the other. As we approached some thick hemlocks, the monitor beeped louder and louder and I was certain we would finally see the elusive buck. It was not to be.

Before we could spot the deer, the radio transmission began indicating the buck was moving. Twenty-five deer came out of

Once hunting pressure increases, bucks will seldom chase does during daylight hours. Rutting activity will continue, but under the cover of darkness.

the woods but none of us saw the collared buck. At first we thought he stayed in the ten-acre woods but we soon learned he escaped undetected between the watchers. Later we managed to pick up his signal from another nearby woods. The scene was incredible. We had two radio transmitters to pinpoint the buck's location, plus five avid deer hunters, and we were unable to see the buck. To top it all off, the buck stayed within a quarter mile of where he had been throughout the previous deer season. This illustrates what hunting nocturnal whitetails is all about.

So, contrary to popular belief among hunters, bucks do not move out of the country when hunting pressure increases. The collared buck we have here is an example, as are the other adult bucks in the study. Also, there have been many telemetry studies conducted over the years throughout North America that indicate that whitetails do not abandon their core range during hunting season. Bucks simply hunker down, find the thickest cover possible, and limit their movements to only nighttime or the fringes of daylight.

For years I attempted to hunt deer throughout gun season the same way I did during bow season. Though I killed a buck every year, most were yearlings. It wasn't until I changed tactics that I consistently killed older class whitetails. The big reason for this was learning the habits of mature bucks. Remember, they become nocturnal because of pressure. Also, their maturing causes them to be secretive, almost giving the appearance that they plan their every move. Though I don't believe for a minute whitetails are capable of a thought process as we know it in humans, I do believe they can adapt to know when and when not to be active. The only time they seem to disregard this fail-safe system is during the first three weeks of November (north of the 38th parallel), when the rut has them in a frenzy, and even then they are cautious about what they do.

HUNTING STRATEGY

To be successful, hunting nocturnal bucks requires that you scout smart for them. For years I hunted the same way the entire deer season. This amounted to hunting the scrape areas I'd found early in the season. The only thing wrong with this was that once the full-blown rut arrived and gun season came in, scraping activity dwindled to almost nothing. Deer sightings also decreased after a couple of days of shotgun season.

My buck sightings and opportunities increased dramatically when I began thinking, "If I were a buck, where would I be hiding during the season?" As might be expected, I began to look intently at the thickest bedding areas I could find. In order to save time and energy, I used aerial photos (as described in Chapter 2) to locate bedding areas. Also, when these areas coincide with the topo map's steep elevation lines, it's an indicator of where deer will be bedded. Note that whitetails love to bed just over an edge where they can see a distance downwind and at the same time have their back to the wind, enabling them to smell danger in the direction they can't see.

Though mentioned in the scouting chapter, I'll reiterate the importance of determining the area's relation to food and water, for it will reveal how a buck moves to and from the bedding area. When a trail is found leading to or from a bedding area, look at the tracks closely. If most or all are heading toward the feeding area, the trail is probably being used in the evening. If the tracks indicate going into the bedding area, the trail is being used in the morning. Knowing their escape routes and how tracks and other sign appear helps in determining an ambush location, as well as in planning hunting strategy. Also, when bucks retreat to bedding areas they do not stop making rutting sign, they merely move their rutting act to the bedroom. This is why I look for old rubs and scrapes when I'm scouting a bedding area in the winter.

I plan my ambush of a nocturnal buck by being as inconspicuous as possible. This means that I do not spend a lot of time in the area. I hang my stands near the bedding area's known escape routes or where sign and cover is thickest. In addition I

With hunting pressure high, bucks will bed the entire day and move only when pushed.

make sure that the stands are hung at least a month before I intend to hunt the area. Because of their size and the amount of noise required to build them, I seldom use permanent stands when hunting nocturnal bucks in thick cover. It's just too risky. If you make too much commotion in a buck's bedroom he'll move out. With the stand in place, I take time to cut several small shooting lanes. And lastly, I make sure I have at least two ways to get into the stand quietly. This point is critical. If you rely on only one entrance and exit route, deer will figure you out in a hurry.

Once the stands are hung it's time to come up with a strategy for hunting the area. During bow season the bulk of my hunting will be in the transition zone, between the bedding and feeding area. However, if the pressure of small game season begins to force nocturnal behavior, I'll start hunting the bedding areas. The key is being able to monitor activity. If sightings drop off in the transition and feeding zones during legal hunting hours, then move to the buck's bedroom.

When gun season opens and the red coats attack the woods, any bucks (including yearlings) that are not already nocturnal become night owls in a heartbeat, or so it seems. When this happens I retreat to the thick confines of the bedding area.

In November of 1993 I traveled to Turtle Lake, Saskatchewan, to hunt with outfitter Bentley Brown. On my trip from the airport

Bentley and I talked about how his hunters had been doing and about my desire to hunt in thick cover where a good amount of rutting activity was present. I explained that I wanted to rattle in a big buck if possible. Brown assured me he had just the spot, an area off the end of a big swamp where a lot of scraping and rubbing had been found.

November 12 dawned with me perched in a big jackpine. About four inches of fresh snow clung to the trees, making it difficult to see very far in any direction. Shortly after daylight I went through my first rattling sequence of the day. Nothing showed. About an hour later a doe moved through the thick brush forty yards away and wandered out of sight. At ten-thirty I went through my second sequence, rattling for about ten minutes. Again, nothing. Knowing Bentley would be checking on me at twelve-thirty, I decided to rattle one more time about quarter of twelve.

With high noon nearly upon me I went through my last rattling sequence of the morning. Within seconds of completing the sequence I heard a branch break behind me. Slowly I turned my head but unfortunately the brush was too thick to see anything. Immediately I heard more branches breaking. Experience told

When bucks turn nocturnal, aggressive hunting tactics are needed. I killed this Saskatchewan buck at high noon by rattling and grunting him within range.

The Cloverleaf Still-hunt

400 YARDS

The cloverleaf still-hunt: One hunter climbs into a tree stand in the heart of a prime bedding area. Then, a lone still-hunter makes a big loop away from the stand hunter, and then comes back. When the still-hunter returns to where he can almost see the stand, he makes another loop, continuing the process until he has gone a full 360 degrees around the stand.

me a buck was raking his antlers in overhanging branches. I also knew it would be foolish to rattle again. In order to see the buck I realized I'd have to rely on my grunt tube. Softly I let out two guttural grunts from the tube. Instantly the buck walked out of some spruce thirty yards away. It was too thick for a shot. He continued to walk and when he got seventy yards away he stepped into a little opening and I squeezed the trigger on my .270. At the rifle's roar the big buck jumped, trotted about thirty-five yards, and piled up.

When I was following the buck in my scope I knew his rack was big, but it wasn't until I walked up to him that I realized just how big. The buck carried eleven countable points and even though he had to be scored as a basic 4X5 (the rack had two stickers) his rack gross scored 162 Boone & Crockett typical.

Neither Brown nor his previous hunters had ever seen this buck. He truly fit the description of a nocturnal animal, one who lived in thick cover and seldom moved. Also, typical of nocturnal bucks this bruiser was active in midday, a point to remember when you pursue secretive bucks. Three things put me in a position to kill this buck. First, a desire to hunt the thickest possible cover, where heavy rutting sign was present. Second, knowing how to rattle and use a grunt tube. Rattling brought him to me but it took the grunt tube to give me the shot. And third, making sure that I was still in the woods at high noon, when nocturnal bucks are often active.

Though stand hunting works well, silent drives can also be productive for hunting nocturnal bucks. Late in the season when it appears all the bucks have left the country, I like to put on what I call my cloverleaf tactic. It works like this. One hunter positions himself in a tree stand in the heart of a prime bedding area. Then, one lone still-hunter proceeds to make big loops from the stand hunter. The still-hunter hunts away from the stand, makes a big loop, then comes back. The still-hunter comes back to where he can almost see the stand, then he makes another loop, continuing the process until he has gone a full 360 degrees around the person in the stand. How far out the loop takes the still-hunter depends on the size of the bedding area, but generally the loop will take in woods about four hundred yards from the stand. If you were to look at this strategy from above it would resemble a four leaf clover, with the stander in the middle.

I've been successful with this technique over the years and in 1993 I killed my biggest gun buck ever on our property using it. About two o'clock in the afternoon I climbed into a prime bedding area stand. Shortly after my good friend, Paul Daniels, began making the cloverleaf loops and by four o'clock had nearly completed the second loop (about 180 degrees). Without realizing it, he jumped a big eight point that trotted by my stand as it tried to escape. One shot from my .12 gauge brought the buck down in his tracks.

When bucks stop moving during the day, still-hunting and drive hunting may be the only ways sightings are possible.

The Staggered Still-hunt

75 to 150 yards

The staggered still-hunt: Two hunters still-hunt single file through a bedding area, anywhere from 75 to 150 yards apart. By still-hunting into the wind or with a crosswind, the lead hunter might jump a deer. The deer will often circle back, giving the second hunter a possible shot.

Though I feel the cloverleaf tactic is best, there are other silent drives that work well. One is to have two hunters still-hunt single file through a bedding area, anywhere from seventy-five to one hundred-fifty yards apart. By still-hunting into the wind or with a crosswind, the lead hunter may jump a deer that will often circle back, giving the second hunter an opportunity for a shot.

Another popular silent drive for nocturnal bucks is to have two to four hunters still-hunt toward each other in a known bedding area. The key is to move slowly and quietly. Also, whenever silent drives are conducted, blaze orange is a must to prevent accidents.

chapter 8

THE SECOND RUT?

When looking through old hunting magazines I find various articles dealing with the whitetail's second rut. Title after title suggests that the second rut is as good as the first for bagging a nice-racked buck. Most of the articles are written in such a way as to make a whitetail hunter want to pass up hunting November's peak in favor of December's "rage in the woods." Are these writings fact, hype, or a figment of some writer's imagination?

I have to admit that over the years I've been fascinated by the possibilities of hunting the whitetail's second rut. After all, I grew up reading numerous accounts of hunting a whitetail rut after most deer hunters exited the woods in early December. Now, after more than twenty-five years of serious hunting I'm beginning to wonder just how big the so-called second rut really is.

This questioning didn't just happen overnight. For years my field observations didn't match with what I was reading. And with each passing year I truly wondered why I wasn't seeing the frenzied second rut in December that writers were alluding to. I wondered...what am I missing?

This is not to say that I have not witnessed rutting activity from mid-December to early January, for I have. As one of a handful of deer photographers who have captured nearly all aspects of whitetail behavior, I've been fortunate to have photographed a fair amount of rutting activity during what hunters call the second rut. This has ranged from rubbing, to chasing, to the actual breeding. However, the whitetail behavior I've witnessed during the last ten years doesn't come close to rivaling the rutting activity I observe in early to mid-November each year. Why?

There are many reasons for this and all seem to play a part in determining the amount of rutting activity that occurs after

Though some chasing goes on, most of the does have been bred by December in the North. Only a few does and doe fawns keep bucks interested.

mid-November's peak. Fortunately biologists are beginning to shed some light on the rutting aspect of a whitetail's life, like never before. During the course of putting this book together, I contacted some of the most respected whitetail biologists in America. No two seemed to agree on everything, but a common bond they all shared was a doubt for the so-called second rut, at least in the hunter's context.

Well-known whitetail biologist John Ozoga from Michigan stated, "I don't think I like the term second rut. I suppose there could be one in some situations, but I'm not sure it exists the way most envision it. In reality, if plotted, the rut would be a curve with a couple blips in it." Ozoga went on to share that so many things go into determining whether there is a condensed or a protracted rut.

He feels that the rut in northern Michigan is condensed, due to the cold conditions that exist there. However, in southern Michigan, he feels the whitetail rut is longer because conditions allow yearling does and fawns to come into estrus and be bred in December and January.

Throughout our conversation Ozoga kept referring to a "window of breeding activity" to explain the length of the rut. He defined it by saying, "In nature fawns need to be born on schedule for them to survive. In the northern climates, like Michigan, this means late May and early June. As a result, the further north one goes the narrower the window of breeding activity. In the southern climates where temperatures are warmer, the window of breeding activity doesn't need to be as small. Therefore, in such places the breeding is often drawn out more and in some portions of the whitetail range occur year round."

Another respected biologist, Grant Woods from South Carolina, had similar feelings to Ozoga when it came to the second rut. He said, "I don't believe in a first, second, or third rut because the age class and sex ratio in the majority of deer herds is so poor. My findings show that when sex ratios get out of balance and a herd has few mature bucks in that area, the rut is strung out and often lasts over one hundred days. When this happens all kinds of problems occur and the quality of the herd drops significantly.

"However, when a herd is fine tuned, meaning good age structure, sex ratio, and nutrition, the whitetail rut is very condensed and often lasts less than fifty days. You also find the most rutting sign in a fine tuned herd. On one property I manage there is a one to one buck to doe ratio, and we've recorded 3,000 rubs per square mile in this area. Conception in this area is tight and the rut lasts roughly forty-four days. Interestingly the property next door has a doe to buck ratio of seven to one,

Bucks are still interested in does but with their testosterone level dropping, food is often a greater priority than sex.

As winter sets in bucks continue to rub their antlers and will continue to do so until they are shed.

and the peak of the rut is a month later and strung out over one hundred days."

The New York State Department of Environmental Conservation is currently conducting a study of reproductive and conception dates in two of its deer management units. This study fits Woods' comments concerning the length of the rut when doe to buck ratios are out of balance. With an adult doe to adult buck ratio of approximately nine to one, the breeding dates of the sample carcasses collected show that the does were bred between November 12 and January 25, making for a protracted rut.

In theory an adult buck should be able to breed between four and seven adult females (Jackson 1973). So, when doe to buck ratios are high the adult bucks simply cannot breed all the does when they come into estrus in mid-November. As a result many does cycle out and come into estrus twenty-eight days later.

With sex ratios out of balance three things occur, especially in the northern states where hunting pressures are intense. First, many bucks are killed during the November rut, leaving few to service the does that come into estrus during December's second rut. Second, with a protracted rut the bucks that survive

With few available does to breed, bucks are more interested in food. They also begin to form bachelor groups again.

November's rut and hunting pressure are often greatly stressed by an abundance of estrous does. And in most cases there are not enough bucks to go around and some does are not bred. When this happens many bucks have a difficult time surviving the winter, especially one such as the blizzard of 1993 that hit many eastern states. Lastly, when the doe to buck ratio really gets out of sync, rutting activity and associated sign diminish greatly. This and a buck's decreased desire to breed are two of several key reasons why hunting the second rut is so difficult.

No doubt many hunters will question that a buck has a decreased desire to breed in December. In many cases this is relative and depends on the individual buck. But research (Lambiase 1972) shows that sperm production extends from mid-August through March. During this time the number of sperm per ejaculation increased through October, peaked in mid-November, dropped almost in half by mid-December, then declined at a slower rate thereafter. This sheds light on why bucks go into a rutting frenzy as mid-November and the peak of the rut approaches. It also illustrates why the chase phase of the whitetail rut with its associated rutting activity is such a good time to hunt.

Lambiase's research also shows why less rutting activity takes place in December, even though many does are in estrus. In addition Mother Nature also plays another card during the period known as the second rut. During November's rut white-tailed bucks go progressively from sleek, fat-laden specimens to worn down mirrors of what they were. As a result a white-tailed buck's survival mode kicks in during early December. Rather than constantly chasing, they begin to calm down and start eating, trying to regain the body weight they lost in November. Unfortunately, not all bucks are able to restore lost body reserves and the rut and subsequent winter takes its toll and death prevails.

Because survival is the main objective, a buck becomes a different creature in December and early January. Oh, he will still breed, and often does, but generally he isn't out looking for does the way he was in November. Rather, he feeds, rests, and takes what comes his way.

I've seen this scenario played out so many times during photo and hunting sessions. When December arrives the entire deer family group begins gravitating toward known food sources, such as cornfields or cedar swamp yarding areas. Regardless, the main objective of bucks and does is food, food, food. As a result, trying to hunt November's scrape and rub lines is for the most part a waste of time. I have been able to observe what happens at this time while photographing in New York's Adirondack Mountains during December.

I had gone to a known whitetail wintering area with the intent of photographing some bucks before the severe cold of January set in and they shed their antlers. The early December snows had arrived and so had the deer. All together about thirty does and five or six bucks were frequenting the area, trying to bulk up on as much food as possible. On the second day I was there it was obvious a doe was in estrus. The biggest buck was following her around, but not in an overly aggressive manner. The other bucks, though at times interested, did not join in. Rather, they were more content to bed, rest, and feed.

Though the buck finally bred the doe, he spent more time eating and resting than anything else. On occasion he would give a low guttural grunt if another buck came too close. He never exhibited aggressive behavior or attempted scraping activity. And only once did he bother rubbing a tree. It was almost as if all the bucks knew the doe needed to be bred but no one much cared who did it. I can assure you, had it been mid-November the scene would have been different.

Another example of mid-December (second rut) activity took place several years ago, but is characteristic of previous experiences and worth sharing. I remember the day well, it was December 9, and about five inches of snow covered the ground. In the morning I sat overlooking a stream that runs through our property. About ten o'clock I heard what sounded like deer chasing each other. Unfortunately the sound told me the deer were out of range and not coming closer. After another hour of silence passed, I headed home.

At about three o'clock, with only two hours of light left I headed back to the same area with my eight-year-old son, Aaron, hoping to see some deer. We didn't have to wait long. Fifteen minutes into our sit I could hear two bucks sparring about a hundred yards from us. Within minutes, with the sparring still going on, four does moved down through the woods and out of sight. Not far behind a six point buck followed. Though the sparring grew louder I could tell it hadn't reached the aggressive point yet. The bucks were coming closer. Aaron was loving every minute of it as we sat huddled in our ground blind surrounded by hemlock boughs.

With twenty minutes of daylight left we spotted the four does coming back through the woods toward us, with the yearling buck in tow. They took their time while feeding on hemlock boughs. All this time we could still hear the other bucks sparring. I whispered to Aaron that I was going to let the does and buck pass by as I hoped the sparring bucks were bigger. Not five minutes after they were out of sight, the two combatants came into view and continued their sparring match in a small creek about

Until their antlers are shed, bucks spar with each other in order to maintain their pecking order within the herd.

During the post-rut deer are more apt to be on the move during midday. Rather than breaking for lunch, hunters should hunt through the noon-time hours.

thirty yards from us. Through my scope I could see one was a yearling and the other a heavy six point, probably a 2-1/2-year-old buck. I decided that neither was big enough so we sat and watched their every move. In fading light I brought my grunt tube to my mouth and blew on it twice. At first the bucks ignored the sound but two more grunts got their attention and the bigger buck started in our direction. Before the episode was over he stood fifteen scant paces in front of our blind, trying to figure out what was calling to him. As darkness crept in, he turned and walked off to join his sparring buddy.

Though these two bucks exhibited a small amount of rutting activity, they showed no interest in the four does that fed past as they sparred. It was obvious that they were more interested in "horse play" than sex. Again, had it been November I'm sure the behavior would have been different. These and many other experiences have left me doubting the hype about the second rut.

I am an opportunist when it comes to hunting the time right after November's rut. Though does will be bred during this time I know behavior will be much different. As a result I intensely hunt food sources close to thick cover. Note the last sentence well because it's the heart and soul of hunting the late season or second rut. By concentrating on food sources and bedding areas I'm able to get close to doe groups and the bucks that have survived the firearms season. Remember, does, and particularly bucks need to gain and maintain body weight to survive the winter, so everything else takes a back seat to food--even sex. Also, in the North, where winter has begun, there will be more midday activity during this time, so hunting between 10 a.m. and 2 p.m. will be particularly productive.

As I alluded to in Chapter 6 on calling and rattling, I find rattling during this time to be marginal at best because there is little competition among bucks, mainly because few survive gun season. When I do rattle late in the season, I make more of a sparring noise than the noises I would make if I were simulating a full-blown fight. Seldom will two bucks really go at it after the flurry of the rut is past, so I find less noise to be better. However, I find grunting to be successful after November and use the tube the same way I do in November.

So, are we expecting too much from the second rut? My experience says yes. There's no question that it's a great time to hunt, one of my favorite times to be in the woods. But in spite of some does being bred, the true rutting activity of November is long gone. Larry Marchinton, one of the best deer researchers and hunters in the business, made an interesting comment to me. He said, "I'm not a believer in the second rut...North or South. It is basically a writer's and hunter's phenomenon." And you know what? I tend to agree with him.

chapter 9

DECOYING FOR WHITETAILS

A few years ago I made the following statement to a group of people. "Other than in the area of research there is nothing new on the whitetail horizon." Boy, was I wrong! Shortly after that I began photographing and hunting with whitetail decoys and quickly realized the excitement of "deercoying." Since my first experiment with decoys I've been able to witness some incredible interactions between real and "fake" whitetails.

Of all the techniques available to hunters, deercoying is the hottest thing to come along in the last twenty-five years. For centuries native Americans used decoys to harvest wild game. Unfortunately their craft of decoying was not passed on to the early settlers. Because of this, today's hunters are forced to learn decoying as they go.

There is more involved in decoying than merely purchasing a decoy and taking it into the woods. First, you have to decide whether you want to use a buck or doe decoy. Then the decoy needs to be made woods ready. With these two things completed the setup (the most critical aspect) must be thought out.

When I began deercoying, about the only decoy on the market was the Flambeau upright doe. Now the market is being flooded with all kinds of models to choose from, ranging from silhouette styles to full-bodied models. Though I've had great success from both doe and buck decoys, I prefer to use a doe decoy when hunting the rut because of its ability to be a real buck magnet. Also, I've had greater response to them than with buck decoys. It's not only important to buy a decoy that is anatomically correct but also one that is durable, because bucks have no mercy on their foe. As you can see from the photos, bucks literally try to kill the decoy when they become frustrated.

Most manufacturers handle the buck decoy provision by supplying an antler kit for the doe decoy. Though these will work, I find that most antler kits don't provide large enough antlers. Unlike a doe decoy, where the buck responds to the decoy's sex, a buck decoy works differently. When a buck spots a buck decoy, it focuses on two qualities in the decoy. First, the decoy's antler size, and second its body size. These two things along with a buck's individual behavior determine dominance in the buck population. So, for a buck decoy to be successful the antlers and body size must be representative of the rack and body size of deer in the area a person hunts. If the decoy's antlers and body are too large or small, interaction will not be good. For this reason I find that a 120 class set of antlers works best on a buck decoy throughout most of North America. Though buck decoys can work well in the rut, my best buck decoy results have come in the pre- and post-rut period.

Once the decoy is purchased, work to get it woods ready. Make sure that there is some way of anchoring it so that a buck or the wind doesn't knock it over. Flambeau's doe decoy and some others have eyelets near the hooves so that a tie down can be put in place. I anchor my doe decoys with 10-inch long spikes with the end bent over. In a way they resemble tent pegs. Also, I assemble the decoy when I get within 150 yards of where I intend to hunt. Remember this tip because decoys can be noisy (most are made of plastic) and should not be put together at the hunting site for this reason. If an anchoring provision isn't built into the decoy make your own. Also, make sure no exposed skin comes in contact with the decoy. I always hunt with cover-up laden clean clothes and always cover my hands with gloves when carrying a decoy into a hunting area.

I've had many bucks walk right by a decoy in brush so the decoy must be set up in fairly open cover. This point is vital because the decoy must be seen to be effective. Over the years I've found that the edge of a food source or a natural funnel in open woods works best.

Using a grunt tube is an excellent way to get a buck to spot a positioned decoy. Often, if the buck is walking out of range of the decoy I'll blow a couple doe bleats or buck grunts. When a buck hears this he'll look in the direction of the decoy and often come to investigate.

The bottom line in deercoying is that a buck becomes so focused on the decoy that it ignores everything around him, allowing the hunter to move and make the shot. This is the crux of decoying, aside from its entertainment. The following two sequences are two of many buck/decoy interactions I've photographed over the years and are classic examples of what happens when a white-tailed buck encounters a decoy.

DOE DECOYING

This sequence of a white-tailed buck and Flambeau doe decoy was taken just before the peak of the rut in New York in 1991. The day was windless, overcast, with the temperature about fifty degrees--just right for hunting rut-crazed bucks. Around

This eight point buck approached from the decoy's rear and paused for a few moments before circling the "doe."

While circling the decoy, the buck continually checked it out, smelling its ear, staring at it...

and using different body language to try to make it move.

three in the afternoon this eight point approached the decoy in typical form, making his final approach from the rear. After pausing a few seconds near the decoy's flank, he began to slowly circle the "doe" for a better look. He was totally transfixed by the decoy and seemed to ignore everything around him. Though cautious, the buck smelled the decoy's ears and several times made bluffing gestures to try and get it to move. After the buck circled the decoy he stood behind it and bobbed his head up and down as he tried to get it to move. Finally the buck attempted to mount and breed the decoy, only to slide off. This was the decoy's downfall. Who knows what went through the buck's mind, but being unable to breed the "doe" he became furious and attempted to destroy his "lover." Unfortunately he momentarily got his antler caught in a hole in the belly of the decoy before freeing himself and running off. The whole process of his approaching the decoy, circling it, mounting it, and goring it took less than two minutes.

If I'm bowhunting with a doe decoy I set it up roughly 15 to 25 yards from my tree stand so that I'm looking at the decoy's rump when I'm in the stand. An example of this can be seen in the photo next to this chapter's title page. I've positioned doe decoys many ways and find that this works best because most bucks will come into the decoy from the side or the rear, often giving a broadside shot. Also, make sure there are shooting lanes on either side of the decoy because when a buck stretches

After the buck made one complete circle, he tried to mount the decoy.

The buck became upset at being "tricked."

He took out his frustration on the decoy by trying to destroy it.

to smell the "doe" his vitals will be a good distance from the decoy (as some of these photos illustrate). On more than one occasion I've had bucks come into a doe decoy and had their vital area blocked by a sapling or branch.

When rifle or shotgun hunting over a buck or doe decoy, positioning is not as critical and it makes little difference whether the decoy is facing toward or away from you. In most cases I place the decoy (buck or doe) less than 100 yards from my stand if I'm using a firearm.

BUCK DECOYING

Though I don't use a buck decoy as much as a doe decoy, I've had some good successes using a Montana Critter Company decoy over the years. This sequence of a tremendous buck and a Montana Critter decoy was taken in Ohio at the tail end of 1993's rut and shows how powerful the dominance factor can be among white-tailed bucks. When I set up the decoy in a small clearing next to a brushy ravine, the temperature was around 45 degrees with a slight drizzle falling.

About two hours after daylight the big buck stepped out from the edge of the woods and stared at the decoy. After a few brief moments he headed toward the decoy in a stalking stiff-legged manner. During the entire approach the big buck's body lan-

After setting up the Montana Critter Company decoy, a big buck came out of the woods and approached the buck decoy in an aggressive manner...as if to be saying, "I'm going to kill you." This behavior is typical of interaction between two big bucks.

guage seemed to be saying one thing to the decoy..."I'm going to kill you." Characteristic of what I'd observed in the past, the buck walked by the decoy and approached it from the side. In one powerful thrust the buck rammed his antlers into the decoy's left hindquarter. Even though I'd anchored the decoy with a heavy post, the big non-typical buck knocked it over with ease and began viciously attacking it.

Unfortunately, once the decoy hit the ground the tall grass obstructed much of what was happening and didn't give me a good camera angle. With grunting and grinding going on I had to make a decision. I could stay put and hope for the best or I could try to move my long telephoto lens to a better angle knowing that I might spook the buck if I did. I decided to gamble. With the buck occupied mauling the decoy, I quietly moved to a different position. The gamble paid off.

The scene was awesome and I shot film as fast as I could. Through the lens the buck looked like a weight lifter working out at Gold's Gym. As he ground his massive antlers into the neck and antlers of the decoy I could see him break the decoy's left antler. In a quick move, like a wrestler's takedown, the buck jumped across the decoy, turned, and drove his antlers into the decoy's flank. Then with several powerful jerks and thrusts, the buck threw the decoy and post into the air. I couldn't believe what I was seeing; he was tossing the decoy around like a balloon.

I now had a problem on my hands. I don't know if you've ever priced a Montana Critter Company decoy but let me just say they retail for over $500. With each passing second I realized the decoy was moving closer and closer to the point of never being usable again. And I wanted to use it another day.

Feeling I'd taken some great images, I decided to try and spook the buck in order to save the decoy. I began hollering and waving my hands to get the buck to leave. For the first few moments the buck ignored my gesturing, then stopped and looked in my direction. Through the lens I saw him eerily looking at me as I took one last photo. He looked down at his fallen victim, then casually walked off.

In these two photos the big buck circles the decoy and runs into it, knocking it over. The amount of power he exhibited was incredible.

When I inspected the decoy I found it had held up better than I thought. In spite of a broken left antler and many puncture holes, I'd be able to use it again. You might ask, what are the chances of this happening again? Well, as these two photo essays show, no two buck/decoy encounters are identical but they are almost always predictable, which is the beauty of deercoying.

The setup for bowhunting over a buck decoy should be just the opposite of a doe decoy. In other words, have the buck decoy

Being unable to photograph due to high grass, I gambled and moved to a small ravine where I was able to get a better photography angle. I shot film fast as the big buck tried to kill the decoy. He drove his antlers into the foam animal with tremendous force, doing considerable damage to the decoy.

Realizing the buck was going to destroy my decoy, I began shouting in an attempt to get him to stop. For a brief moment I thought he was going to come my way before he walked off.

facing you or quartering slightly toward you. Unlike with a doe decoy, a buck almost always approaches a buck decoy from the front, as the sequence illustrates. When this happens you should have a great chance for a quartering away shot as the buck walks slowly by your stand.

There is a lot being written about using multiple decoys when hunting. Though this type of strategy has merit, it isn't practical unless conditions are perfect. This is because decoys are bulky and noisy and require a lot of effort to get them and your other equipment into place. So, it's best to stick with using one decoy. If you want to use two, I suggest using one upright decoy and one bedded doe decoy.

To ensure there is a moment of truth, a good cover-up is a must when deercoying. Once the decoy is positioned spray it heavily with a good cover-up. If there is any human odor on a decoy, the party is over. So, working the wind and using a good cover-up are essential.

SAFETY

Perhaps the most important aspect of hunting with a decoy is the safety side of deercoying. Safety should never be taken lightly when hunting over a decoy. Personally I'll never use a decoy when I'm hunting from the ground in bow or gun season. Angles are critical when using a decoy, and dodging arrows and bullets is not my idea of what deer hunting is all about. When a person begins using a decoy, they are struck by the fact that the decoy looks so real when placed in a natural setting. I can't begin to tell you the number of times I've sat in a tree stand, started to daydream, then thought I was looking at a real deer when I looked at a decoy. It's difficult to get used to having a decoy in front of you.

To carry this one step further, I take extreme measures when decoying during gun season, wherever I am. It's important to put some blaze orange on the decoy whenever it's moved. An example of how dangerous deercoying can be comes from a real account of Canada's 1993 deer season. This story did not happen where I hunted but with a different Canadian outfitter. On a crisp November morning during the peak of the rut, the outfitter dropped one of his hunters off at a stand where a Montana Critter Company buck decoy was being used. The decoy carried a 160 class set of antlers. After dropping the hunter off at the decoy location, he proceeded and dropped off another hunter at a stand not far away. Around midmorning the hunter hunting with the decoy killed a big buck as it approached the decoy. After inspecting the kill the hunter climbed back onto his stand to wait for the outfitter to return.

The hunter who was hunting nearby heard the shot and came to see what his companion had killed. When he got close to where he thought the stand was, he spotted a big buck in a clearing. Not realizing it was a decoy he brought his gun to his shoulder and shot three times before it dawned on him something was wrong. He had hit the decoy with all three shots. Needless to say the two hunters and outfitter were quite shaken by what took place and it illustrates the danger of using a decoy during firearms season.

"Deercoying" is without question the newest and perhaps the best deer hunting technique to appear in a long time. However, it's still in its infancy, with much to be learned. Because of the variations in a buck's personality, one never knows whether he will ignore the decoy, attack it, or run away. It's been my experience that in about thirty percent of the cases deer ignore, or worse yet, run from a decoy. Last year I lost the chance of killing a 140 class nine point in Texas when he spooked and ran before ever giving me a shot. So, it's far from foolproof. The key is that a white-tailed buck has to be in the right frame of mind in order for deercoying to work.

chapter 10

WEATHER FRONTS AND WHITETAILS

Hunters are forever asking me what I think is the most important ingredient in whitetail hunting. Without fail my answer surprises them when I say understanding weather fronts and the weather that accompanies the fronts. I quickly follow up by telling them why I feel this rates as high as scents, scrape hunting, rattling, or the equipment I use.

Down through the years I've come to realize that understanding weather fronts and the weather that precedes or follows can mean the difference between success and failure in the deer woods. Aside from the basic necessities of survival, it's weather that causes an increase in whitetail movement when natural conditions prevail. I'll even go so far as to say that once a deer hunter understands the various hunting techniques, his application of them to weather systems will be a key to success. Certainly, learning how to hunt weather fronts is not the only key for a hunter but the weather systems that accompany a front may dictate the hunting method used on a particular day.

During the course of a year weather causes all kinds of disruptions, and frenzies, in the way whitetails feed and move. Knowing this has made me more and more of a weather watcher during the last fifteen years, especially during deer season. I live in the East, and due to prevailing weather patterns, the upper Midwest's weather takes around eighteen hours to reach our area. So, during the deer season I make it a point to watch the Midwest's weather so I'll know what kind of weather is approaching. I also watch the barometer to see if it is falling as the front moves closer.

Learning to read prevailing weather patterns can put a hunter in position to kill a big buck when the weather changes.

Unlike humans, whitetails and other wild creatures have built-in mechanisms to alert them to impending weather changes. Whitetails are able to detect when the barometric pressure is falling, even if the sky is clear. They truly know when things are in the process of changing and their feeding habits increase dramatically before bad weather arrives. Over the years it's been my experience that whitetails tend to move more when the barometer is moving, in either direction, than when it is steady. I've observed that whitetails do not like to move when the barometer is low and steady, except during the rut. During this time you'll usually find periods of high humidity with fog, haze, rain, and wet snow making up the weather system. When this happens whitetails become secretive, especially during periods of dense fog. However, during the rut whitetails feed and move more than most people think when the weather is less than ideal. When there are periods of light drizzle, and the rut is on, I expect some of my best whitetail hunting.

During the rut bucks will be on the move during periods of rain, providing it isn't a driving rain.

Just prior to a storm, whitetails will be on the move and feeding. This is a great time to be in the woods.

Dave Buckley of West Valley, New York, is known as one of America's top canoeists. He's also an outstanding bowhunter who spends much of the fall pursuing New York's farmland bucks. Over the years he's kept accurate journals on all aspects of the whitetail's life and weather that are worth noting. "As far as barometric pressure is concerned I believe wildlife reacts more to the rate of pressure change than to the direction of such change. It's pretty well agreed that animals will feed very actively before an approaching storm. The morning before the blizzard of 1993 we saw many deer at our feeder. The next day the blizzard hit. The barometer was extraordinarily low and nothing moved for several days. Also, with a rapidly rising barometer, I have observed that deer seem more active."

An example of what takes place when the barometer falls rapidly and a weather front moves in can be illustrated from one of my recent deer seasons. New York's 1988 shotgun season had been typical for this area. After a flurry of deer activity during the first few days of the season, fewer and fewer deer sightings were taking place as the last week of the season arrived. The last Monday of the season was pretty much a repeat of the previous ten days with little activity. On Tuesday afternoon the temperature dropped and snow began falling. With it came high winds, making hunting difficult. Rather than brave the elements I decided to sit out the storm.

The next morning dawned clear and cold, with two inches of fresh snow on the ground--perfect for deer hunting. I decided to take a stand near a well-used stream crossing. I wasn't in my blind long enough to chill down before I heard snow crunching on the other side of the stream. I brought my gun to my shoulder and waited. In single file a doe and two fawns crossed the stream, walked past my stand and out of sight. Within twenty minutes, two more does and a spike buck followed their trail. I decided to pass on the spike buck hoping something bigger would come by.

For the next hour the woods became quieter as only chipmunks and gray squirrels moved about. As the sun rose, the

When a storm finally arrives whitetails will bed and wait for the storm to pass before becoming active again.

woods warmed and the freshly fallen snow began to melt. Behind me I heard a twig snap in the direction the does, fawns, and spike buck had gone an hour before. At first I wasn't sure what was coming but through the snow laden branches I began picking up patches of brown. I brought the shotgun to my shoulder and peered through the scope. Five does and fawns and what appeared to be the spike buck I passed up were feeding back past me.

Just as the group was about to go out of sight I picked up more movement. Another deer was trailing them. In one motion I threw my gun to my shoulder and scoped the deer. Sun reflected off antler tines and immediately I knew the buck was worth shooting. As he passed by thirty yards from me, I clicked off the safety and pulled the trigger. At the 12 gauge's roar the buck jumped and ran twenty yards before falling within view.

As I sat in the woods admiring the buck, I reflected on all the deer movement I had seen in the first two-and-one-half hours that morning. It was obvious that the sudden change in weather

For the hunter willing to withstand the elements, hunting in poor weather can often provide great opportunities, especially right after the rain or snow stops.

had caused all the movement, for there were no other hunters in the woods.

It is important for the hunter to realize that it is not the sudden drop in temperature that often accompanies these fronts that causes whitetails to head for the thickest cover. Rather, it is the unsettled weather associated with the leading edge of the low pressure front that causes movement, with the greatest movement occurring if the barometric pressure drops rapidly. With few exceptions little deer movement will occur once the front arrives. Then, as the front passes through, and the weather returns to normal, whitetails and other wildlife start to move again in search of food.

When the front finally moves on and it clears off, deer hunters will almost always find some of their best hunting. If a hunter is in the woods within a few hours of the front moving out of an area, the hunting can be fantastic.

Unfortunately few whitetail hunters have the flexibility to take to the woods when weather conditions are best. Most hunters simply must wait for a day off and hope they hit it right, unless of course, they know how to hunt in any kind of condition. When fronts are coming and going, many types of strategies can be successful for hunting whitetails.

If you know the barometer will be falling and a low pressure system is coming, your best bet is to hunt the feeding areas, scrapes, and natural funnel zones. It's at this time that whitetail activity will be high prior to the front's arrival. Once the front arrives, stand hunting may be futile as deer activity will be at a minimum, unless the rut is full blown. It is during these lows (when the storm has arrived) that still-hunting may be at its best. Usually the rain or snow will cover any noise made underfoot. Also, the wind associated with a storm or low pressure system will help to cover any noise you might make. Even swirling wind can be used to your advantage, as whitetails will often have difficulty locating the source of man's scent. If you ever had a desire to be a still hunter, this is the time to try.

When the lows are present whitetails will most certainly be in thick cover or in their traditional bedding areas. Storms force them to seek as thick a cover as possible and they will not leave such areas unless they are forced to. It is truly a time that the hunter must hunt the bedding areas to be successful.

Once the front has begun to move out of an area, wildlife activity increases as the weather returns to normal. Whitetails will then move to feeding areas to catch up on the feeding times they missed. Because they're playing catch-up with their systems, they may be in a feeding frenzy for two or three days depending on how long the storm lasted. It's at this time that many deer hunters find their greatest successes.

For years Steve Moak, from Voorheesville, New York, has been successful hunting big whitetails along the weather fronts. The 39-year-old Moak has killed over fifty whitetails, fourteen of

Hunting the natural funnels and food sources can be productive just before or after a front has moved through.

which have net scored between 130 and 168 Boone and Crockett. When discussing weather fronts he told me, "I've hunted Alberta, Colorado, Manitoba, Saskatchewan, New Brunswick, New York, Minnesota, and Texas for whitetails. Even though the climates of each are distinct, the passage of weather fronts in each location can provide an excellent opportunity to take a trophy whitetail.

"In most areas I've found that bucks are more active after the passage of a front. They will move before a front, but where there is heavy hunting pressure, like much of the East, this movement will be nocturnal. However, in many cases I've seen excellent daylight buck movement as a storm wound down and passed on. In Manitoba a couple seasons ago, it snowed one day until around midnight and then it calmed. The next morning, even with the temperature at -15 degrees, I found tracks everywhere in the snow as I headed to my stand. Before I could get to my stand I saw seven deer and killed a big ten point that scored 158 Boone and Crockett.

"In four previous years of hunting Alberta and Manitoba I had never seen this many deer in one morning; in fact it was more than I had seen during a week of hunting there some seasons. I've found that the passage of a front, coupled with rutting activity, can be a magical combination."

If the rut is combined with weather fronts, whitetail hunting is at its finest. When the front is either coming or going the does are busy feeding. This, coupled with the continual movement of bucks, makes hunting exciting. Over the years I've found hunting scrapes particularly productive when these two factors line up. If possible the hunter should stay on stand all day because buck activity will be continual. Midday can be particularly productive as the bucks make their rounds.

One of the reasons I'm not too fond of guided whitetail hunts to other parts of the country is because of the impact weather fronts have on deer hunting. Usually such hunts are short, four to six days in most cases, so the hunter is at the mercy of what Mother Nature deals him in the way of weather. Because of the short duration, unfamiliar country, and guides that often know less than the hunter they are guiding, such hunts can be frustrating. I've been on great guided hunts and others I'd rather not remember. However, I've found successes in all the hunts by being able to apply knowledge from years of being in the woods.

A smart deer hunter will prepare himself to be his own weather forecaster in the field. One doesn't necessarily have to be near a radio or have a barometer to forecast the weather. If a hunter can identify cloud types it is possible to tell whether a storm front is coming. Altocumulus clouds are often a sign of unsettled weather or an approaching front. Generally they are seen as an extensive sheet of regularly arranged cloudlets, white and gray, and somewhat rounded. If they are found gathering on the north or northwest horizon and accompanied by a

Once a front has moved through and the weather returns to normal, bucks will be on the move, perhaps for several days.

south or southwest wind, it's an indication the barometric pressure is falling. When this condition prevails whitetails will usually be in a feeding mode.

When the front actually arrives the cloud cover will usually be in the form of stratus clouds. These are the clouds that produce drizzle, snow, and are gray and ominous looking. When these clouds appear whitetail activity will diminish in most cases and trying to hunt them from stands will be almost futile, unless, of course, the rut is at its peak. If you are on a guided hunt you may want to still-hunt, regardless of what the guide wants you to do.

On the other hand, clearing skies signal that a front may be on its way out. Also, slight breezes from the north or northwest and very high and scattered cumulus clouds can be confirmation that a front is leaving the area. When this happens whitetails will again be on the move to their source of food.

If more whitetail hunters studied weather and weather fronts as much as they do scents and the rut, success rates would no doubt be higher. Mastering the various techniques associated with whitetail hunting is a challenge but one thing is certain; knowing how to hunt the weather fronts can add precious memories to the hunting experience.

chapter 11

WHITETAILS NORTH AND SOUTH

North America. Wow! Can there be a more beautiful place on earth? I doubt it. I've been blessed to have seen nearly every portion of it pursuing wildlife and whitetails with bow, gun, and camera. It's truly Eden and the beautiful part of it is that white-tailed deer inhabit nearly every part of it. Over the years I've chased whitetails from Nova Scotia to the Mexican border to the wilds of Saskatchewan and have been fascinated by their ability to adapt to whatever man and nature throws at them. For this reason I rank them as North America's top big game animal.

Because of my experiences I'm often asked about hunting whitetails in various parts of the continent. Throughout North America there are many outstanding places to hunt for big white-tailed bucks: Ohio, Illinois, Kansas, Montana, South Dakota, and Maine are but a few places to find a trophy buck. But as good as these locations can be, they're still a long shot for the non-resident hunter.

If I had to pick one place to hunt whitetails, it would be right here on our farm in western New York. As they say, "there's no place like home." But the reality of this is that quality class whitetails are hard to come by in the East. With our area's heavy gun pressure, few bucks live past 2-1/2 years of age. So, next to home where would I go? In spite of all the other so-called hot spots, there are really only two on the continent, Canada in the north and Texas in the south.

I love Saskatchewan and Texas. I've hunted both places several times and the white-tailed bucks found there can take your breath away. They are as different as night and day, one cold and swampy and the other warm and arid. Simply put, hunting

Saskatchewan and Texas is the epitome of what whitetail hunting, North and South, is all about.

CANADA

November in Saskatchewan can be a real human endurance test. I've hunted the province several times and the weather took me to the limit each time. It's no place for the hunter who dislikes snow and cold. But if you want the opportunity of hunting some of the biggest whitetails on the planet, this is the place to go.

Unfortunately hunters going there must contend with more than the cold weather. Good Saskatchewan hunting areas can be hard to find, so choosing an outfitter is critical. I speak from

Though the weather can be bitter, Saskatchewan is the place to go for trophy bucks. This is one of the bucks I killed with Bentley Brown in 1993.

experience, as I've hunted with both good and bad Saskatchewan outfitters. On my first Saskatchewan hunt I liked the country I hunted but the outfitter knew very little about whitetail hunting. As a result I wasted too much time scouting during my six day hunt, and came home empty. The second time around I was smarter, and asked the right questions. I hunted with Bentley Brown, as good a whitetail outfitter as there is in Canada. He knows whitetails and how to hunt them. Consequently I've hunted with him ever since.

Because non-residents can only hunt in the forest region (northern half of the province) of Saskatchewan, the hunting is done, for the most part, in thick forest settings. Brown hunts from tree stands overlooking scrape lines and natural funnels. Also, Saskatchewan isn't a place where a hunter will see a lot of deer. In 1994 I saw only fourteen deer but killed the biggest buck of my life. If you want to see a lot of deer, go to Pennsylvania. But as I said earlier, if you want to have the opportunity to see a great buck, this is where you'll find him.

So, what's hunting Saskatchewan really like? I'll use excerpts from my 1994 Saskatchewan diary to give you an idea.

Day 1 - November 14

As we pulled away from Bentley's lodge the temperature hovered around 18 degrees, with a slight breeze out of the northwest. There were two inches of snow on the ground. I climbed into my stand situated along a seismic line, slipped into my sleeping bag (how I hunt from stands in Canada) and waited for daylight. I liked the location because I could see two hundred yards up and down the line and also into the hardwoods in front of my stand. Shortly after daylight I spotted a deer moving through the hardwoods in front of me. When I scoped him I could see his rack carried ten points. Fortunately the buck fed long enough to give me a good look at his rack...maybe a 130 class. On the last day of the hunt he might be worth shooting, but not today.

Every hour I tried rattling but got no response. By ten o'clock the wind came up and shifted, coming out of the southeast. Around eleven o'clock a wolf began howling off in the distance. Before he was finished, coyotes began to sing not far from my stand. Even with the sleeping bag and cold weather clothing, the subfreezing temperatures began biting at me. I climbed from my stand for ten minutes at noon. Back in the stand I ate lunch. The afternoon was uneventful, with no deer sightings. Day 1 recap: Very cold, one deer sighting, time on stand--ten hours.

Day 2 - November 15

The temperature was 13 degrees above zero as I left the truck and headed into the woods. It was overcast and windless. Today I hunted a funnel area between two swamps. As first light came, I realized that the thickness of the location would limit shots to less than 80 yards. At nine o'clock I rattled for the first time. No response. At ten o'clock I rattled a second time. A few minutes after finishing I picked up movement to my right. With my naked eye I could see a buck making his way toward my stand. Slowly I brought the scope up and decided to pass him. Though he carried eight perfect points, he'd only score about 110.

Nature's call forced me to leave the cozy confines of my sleeping bag and stand at noon. I returned ten minutes later and spent the rest of the day in my perch. A button buck passed by at 2:15 p.m., a small four point at 4 p.m., and a bigger four point at dark. I rattled twice more during the afternoon hours but had no response. Thanks to no wind I weathered the day quite well. Back in camp I found out that fellow New Yorker Don Warren had killed a beautiful 14 pointer in the morning that

Saskatchewan whitetails gliding across a carpet of snow are impressive creatures.

would gross score in the 160s (perfect 6x6 with two stickers). Looking at it in the skinning shed got my hopes up for tomorrow. Day 2 recap: Three bucks, one button buck, ten hours on stand.

Day 3 - November 16

Dawn broke with clear skies and the temperature around 20 degrees. I decided to hunt where I was on day 1 and placed a decoy on the seismic line. This day took me to my physical limit. The wind came up, gusting to thirty miles per hour and by nightfall the temperature was 10 degrees above zero. The wind made it seem like it was -20 degrees. In spite of it I stayed on stand all day. The rut was on and I felt confident that something would be moving. Unfortunately it was not to be. Day 2 recap: Zero deer but plenty of coyote howling. Back in camp Bentley and I discussed where I would go in the morning. Though a hunter had killed a 140+ eight point the week before, he encouraged me to go to a stand he called "Lake 8" because of the sign he was seeing there. Lake 8 it would be.

Day 4 - November 17

Fortunately the wind died down in the night. At dawn the temperature stood at 14 above zero. I had a good feeling that today my luck would change. Bentley walked me to my stand and I waited for shooting light to arrive. The stand was set up in tight conditions, in a mixture of mature aspens and spruce. It looked good and the wind was perfect. An hour after first light a yearling six point moved past my stand. Though I had rattled a half hour before, he didn't appear to be responding to it. Bentley and I had agreed to meet at 1 p.m. to see if I wanted to switch locations for the afternoon's hunt. Around noon I really started to get cold but stuck it out for a few more minutes. At 12:15 p.m. a button buck passed by. As soon as he was out of sight I climbed from the sleeping bag and began walking to the pickup point. My body had really chilled down from the five-hour sit and I needed to warm up. Walking did the trick. I met Bentley at quarter to one and after talking for a couple minutes I headed back to the stand.

Sufficiently warmed, I was set for the afternoon hunt. I didn't have to wait long. Ten minutes after getting settled in my sleeping bag, I picked up movement to my left. I rested the rifle on the stand's railing and put the cross hairs on the deer. My heart skipped a beat when I saw the size of his rack. There was no

In a span of 24 hours last year, Brown's hunters killed these three bucks. This is testimony to the kind of hunting the province offers.

This is why hunters battle the cold of Canada. On November 17 last year I took this 14 pointer that grossed 174 Boone and Crockett.

time to size him up, I just knew he was big. When he walked into a narrow opening I pulled the .270's trigger. At the roar the big buck collapsed. I cranked another shell into the chamber and kept the scope on him, in case I'd have to shoot again. After five minutes I climbed down and walked (more like a run) to the buck. His antlers were beautiful--truly a lifetime whitetail. I spent the rest of the afternoon photographing the buck and checking the sign around the stand. The area was loaded with rubs and scrapes and I could see why Bentley was so high on the location. This day proved to be a banner day for Bentley's hunters. Six hunters put three trophy bucks on the ground. My buck grossed 174 Boone and Crockett but took a back seat to another hunter's giant main frame eight point that grossed 179 Boone and Crockett. Day 4 recap: Two bucks, one button buck. Today was the day!

Though I purchased a second tag (in 1994 two bucks could be taken) I saw no other bucks that interested me during the rest of the week. As mentioned I saw only 14 deer during the week I hunted. However, in 1993 I saw 35 deer and of those, 17 were bucks. In all my trips to Canada about half of the deer I've seen have been bucks, illustrating the great buck to doe ratio that exists there.

To inquire about hunting with Bentley Brown, you can contact him at Box 475, Turtleford, Saskatchewan, Canada, S0M 2Y0. Phone (306)845-2444.

TEXAS

The thing that strikes you most about Texas is that it isn't like you expected it to be. When I first began looking into the prospects of hunting south Texas, I envisioned some forsaken place with impenetrable brush and desert-like conditions. It certainly has the brush and it can be dry, but, oh, does it teem with wildlife. The bird life is incredible and javelinas, coyotes, bobcats, and whitetails are in abundance.

I first started going there to photograph and hunt in 1989 and like Saskatchewan, fell in love with it. But, unlike Canada where deer sightings are limited, the Texas brush country is loaded with whitetails. And on ranches managed for big deer, large racked whitetails can be found in abundant numbers. For this reason the Texas brush country is the ultimate destination for southern whitetail hunting.

I've seen some well-managed operations, such as the Jambers and Zachery ranches, but the Retamosa Ranch, run by the Hefner Appling family is as good as it gets. Many years ago my good friend Erwin Bauer hunted the Retamosa and wrote a story for *Outdoor Life*. In the story Bauer shared his Retamosa

Texas whitetails are beautiful creatures and their antlers are as big as anyplace on the continent.

My best Texas buck from a previous hunt.

experience and how he killed a big white-tailed buck there. From this he nicknamed the ranch "Senderos," meaning the deer there were as big as Texas. He wasn't wrong. When I first saw the Retamosa in 1989 I felt like I was in whitetail heaven. The rut was just kicking in and bucks were running everywhere.

The Retamosa's accommodations are outstanding in every way and the Applings know how to manage for mature deer, especially big racked whitetails. Because of the management success the Applings have had, they offer two kinds of hunts, a Trophy Hunt (for top end bucks) and a Trophy 8 and 9 point hunt for mature eight and nine pointers. I was hunting on the Trophy 8 and 9 point hunt. To give an idea of what hunting south Texas is all about, I'll share from my 1994 diary.

Day 1 - December 16

With overcast skies and a temperature of 70 degrees, Hefner Appling and I set up my decoy before climbing into our stand overlooking a series of senderos (a long narrow opening). As night faded to dawn, deer began showing in three different senderos at the same time. At first shooting light, a 160 class eleven point chased a hot doe through the brush a hundred yards away (this buck is off limits to me). Over the next two hours I saw 15 does and fawns and 7 more bucks in the 125 to 135 Boone and Crockett range--nothing I wanted to shoot. With the temperature rising we headed back to the lodge for lunch. In the afternoon I went to a different stand with Sprague Sommers, one of Hefner's guides, set up the decoy and waited. In spite of it being overcast, the temperature was rising so I didn't expect much movement. I was right. Only a yearling five point and a doe and fawn showed up. Day 1 recap: 21 does and fawns and 11 bucks.

Day 2 - December 17

The temperature dropped in the night to 54 degrees. With overcast and cool conditions I was sure things would be moving. Not so. Though I saw six bucks and nine does and fawns, none were worth shooting. I did witness a "first." Around 8 a.m. a doe and a buck fawn came into the sendero where my decoy was set up. The fawn walked to within fifteen yards of the decoy, postured at it and then worked a scrape's licking branch. Once done he stared at the decoy, then proceeded to rub his buttons on a bush. About the same time a four point stepped into the sendero and walked toward the decoy. What happened next was hard to believe. The button buck and four point began sparring. Did the decoy cause this interaction? I don't know, but in a lifetime of observing deer behavior it's the first time I've ever seen such a display from a fawn. I couldn't help but think what the fawn's mother thought as she watched everything unfold. With activity at a standstill, I headed back to the lodge for lunch at 11:30.

The afternoon sit was different. A cool breeze came up and with the temperature around sixty degrees I saw 16 does and fawns and 6 bucks, one a mature 12 point that I couldn't shoot. Nothing is more frustrating than to see a mature trophy animal and not be able to shoot it. It's kind of like being turned loose in Cabela's with only ten dollars in your pocket. The exciting part was that the rut had kicked in and bucks were on the move. The Texas rut occurs the second half of December. When I got back to camp I discovered that Brian Crawford, from the Albany, New York, area had killed a perfect ten point that would

While I was hunting the Retamosa, Mitch Rhodes and Brian Crawford killed these two bucks, a perfect 10 and 12 point.

gross around 160 Boone and Crockett typical. Day 2 recap: 25 does and fawns, 12 bucks.

Day 3 - December 18

The weather conditions were the same as day two, 54 degrees and overcast at dawn. I hunted until eleven o'clock as bucks were on the prowl. During the sit I saw many does and fawns and bucks. For the first two hours a big 160 class twelve point chased does in and out of the senderos...what a sight, in spite of the fact he was off limits to me. Around 8:30 a.m. I witnessed a first in my life. Four hundred and fifty yards down a fence line from the stand, a big deer jumped the cattle fence. By the time I brought up my binocular, a big 10 point, in the 160 class, went under the fence. Fifteen yards behind him was the biggest buck I've ever seen in the wild. I've scored enough racks in my life to know that the bruiser had at least 200 inches of bone on his head. For starters his G-2s were in the 14-15 inch range with mule deer forks. I couldn't believe what I was looking at. Though the rack was only about 18 inches wide there was "trash" everywhere. An incredible whitetail! An incredible morning sit! When we got back to the lodge for lunch, the camp was admiring a perfect 160 class 12 point killed earlier in the day by Mitch Rhodes of Jacksonville, Florida.

My afternoon hunt turned out better than the morning. With no wind and cool conditions I changed locations, to a stand where another hunter had seen plenty of activity in the morning. Having seen nothing by 4 p.m., I decided to rattle. Immediately after completing the sequence, a perfect 155 class ten point stepped into the sendero where my decoy was set up. Immediately he locked on to it and began approaching from a distance of 200 yards. When he got to within sixty yards of the decoy, he stopped and gave it a hard stare before walking to the edge of the sendero and making a scrape. Once done he continued to stare at the decoy before walking off into the brush. If I was allowed to kill him, I would have in a heartbeat, but again, he wasn't an eight or nine point.

With an hour of light left, a mature buck crossed the sendero about 250 yards from the stand. I picked up my rattle box and rattled loud and hard, trying to bring him toward me and the decoy. Within a minute of finishing, I picked up movement to my right. It was the buck that had crossed the sendero. His upright hair looked like a pincushion as he strutted through the brush. From his position I could see he was going to step into the sendero near the decoy. I wasn't prepared for what happened next. When the big nine point (one I could shoot) hit the sendero, he and the decoy were point blank. The buck never saw the decoy until he hit the opening, and it scared him to death. He turned inside out as he tried to escape and never offered me a shot. Murphy and his infamous law were with me on this one. When I got back to camp Steve Moak from Albany, New York, was driving in with a huge nine point he killed just before quitting time. The buck was a dandy, grossing 156 Boone and Crockett typical. Day 3 recap: 22 does and fawns and 11 bucks.

Day 4 - December 19

Day 4's weather was much the same as the previous two days, overcast and in the 50s at dawn. I changed stands and saw just four deer in the morning, passing up a 125 class eight point. In the afternoon I went back to the same stand and saw one doe and caught glimpses of a mature buck chasing it out of the sendero. At last light, a mature 150 class eleven point fed to within two hundred yards of my stand as the day ended. Day 4 recap: two does and four bucks.

Day 5 - December 20

The temperature had risen in the night and it was humid and 60 degrees as I climbed into my stand, the same location I hunted on the afternoon of Day 3. At first light, four does and fawns fed in one of the senderos. About the time they were going out of sight, the buck that was spooked by my decoy made his way through the high brush two hundred yards from the stand. I decided that if he stepped into the sendero I would shoot him. With rifle ready I waited for the 140 class nine point to give me an open shot. It never happened. Before he hit the sendero he spotted the does and took off on a dead run after them. Fifteen minutes later another mature buck showed up. His right antler had the makings of a big eight point rack. When he turned his head to look in my direction, I discovered he had broken his left antler beam off at the base. I couldn't believe the way my luck was going.

Around 10:30 a.m. a mature buck stepped into a different sendero. I brought up my binocular and glassed the buck. The first thing that struck me was the eight point's spread, easily 26 inches inside. Unfortunately his rack had little mass and his longest point was only six inches long, so I passed. At 11:30, with the temperature near 80 degrees, I climbed from my stand and headed back to camp.

In the afternoon the temperature rose to 94 degrees and the sit was slow. The highlight was the rutting activity of a 2-1/2

What is the Retamosa capable of? Steve Moak of Albany, New York, killed this 196+ buck a couple of years ago and shows what the ranch is capable of. (Steve Moak photo)

year old buck as he chased does in and out of the senderos. The finality of the hunt came with a spectacular Texas sunset, the best of the trip. Day 5 recap: eight does and fawns and four bucks.

Though I didn't kill a buck, my trip to Texas was rewarding. The way I look at it is that I didn't lose, I just ran out of time. I saw some great bucks and learned much about the way the Applings manage the Retamosa. It's truly a place where a hunter can kill the buck of a lifetime. All together I saw six typical bucks I could have easily killed that grossed over 155 Boone and Crockett. Though I knew they were there, I saw no eight or nine pointers that would gross in the 140s. Of the two hunts offered by the Retamosa, the Trophy 8 and 9 point hunt is by far the most difficult.

To inquire about hunting on the Retamosa contact: Hefner Appling, Sr., Appling Farms, P.O. Box 1387, El Campo, TX 77437. Phone (409)543-4301.

chapter 12

FROM THE SHOT TO THE FREEZER

Finding Wounded Deer

It would be nice if every shot a deer hunter took stopped a whitetail in its tracks. Unfortunately this isn't always the case. Too many deer hunters today spend massive amounts of time on the hunting strategies and little on how to recover a whitetail once the shot is taken. This is not to say that hunters are negligent in this aspect of hunting. Lack of experience is the big culprit. Why? First, the modern deer hunter is a loner and seldom hunts with organized groups, such as previous generations did. As a result lone hunters often have a tendency to give up on a track sooner than a group of hunters would. Secondly, deer hunting is one sport where the chance to track a wounded animal doesn't happen often. This may seem hard to believe but if you think about it, the average whitetail hunter only kills about twenty whitetails in his lifetime. Even if you doubled this figure, it still isn't many opportunities when you consider the number of hours, days, or years a person hunts. So, due to lack of tracking experience, deer hunters are not as adept at finding wounded deer as they are at hunting them.

In my mind the process of trailing a whitetail begins five to ten seconds before the shot. Hard to believe? Well, think about what takes place during this time. A hunter's heart tries to jump through his chest as the buck approaches. In addition a hunter's breathing rate becomes irregular as "buck fever" sets in. With his nervous system in overload, every-

Once the shot is fired the trailing process begins.

thing around him becomes a little blurred. It's a phenomenon that only a hunter understands. So, when the moment of truth arrives the last thing a hunter is thinking about is the tracking and recovery process.

Post Shot Analysis

Over the years I've forced myself to do a number of things before I take up the track. First, I stay focused on the animal to see its reaction to the shot. When bowhunting it's often easy to see where the arrow hit, but with gun hunting this is nearly impossible. A buck will usually jump and run from a heart, lung, leg, or grazing shot. If it runs off hard, close to the ground, it often indicates a heart shot. On the other hand it may show no sign of being hit. If a deer is hit in a vital area it seldom runs more than two hundred yards. A gut shot deer usually holds its tail down and hunches up as it runs, while a brain or spinal column shot will drop a deer in its tracks.

So, staying focused on the animal during the shot process is critical.

The second step is to determine where the deer was when the shot was taken and the direction it ran. If you are in a stand make a mental note of these things because when you get on the ground the terrain will look different. Hunting on the ground can be a more complicated process because one tends to unconsciously move after the shot, attempting to follow the running deer. Unfortunately this only causes confusion as to where the deer was standing and where the hunter actually shot from. So, try to stay focused on where you and the deer were. The worst case scenario is to frantically pursue the wounded deer in an unplanned fashion. So, being calm is vital in order to recover a wounded whitetail, especially if it's gut or liver shot.

If you are certain you hit the deer in a vital area and the woods are not full of hunters, stay put for fifteen to twenty minutes. Unfortunately the pressure of opening day of gun season in many portions of the whitetail's range means immediate tracking is a necessity. However, in bow season and under normal conditions, stay put. When I was growing up the standard procedure was to wait an hour before tracking. Over the years I've abandoned this strategy and track

After the shot, stay focused on the animal to see if you can tell where the bullet or arrow struck.

Always approach a downed buck in a cautious manner, making sure it is dead before touching it.

wounded deer according to where I think they are hit and whether I'm bow or gun hunting.

If I'm bowhunting and feel I've hit the buck in a vital area I calm down, get my composure and note landmarks before moving. This usually takes ten to fifteen minutes. The reason I don't wait longer on a vital hit or a leg wound is because a whitetail must bleed to death when hit with an arrow and it must lose 35 percent of its blood for this to happen (2.75 pints in a 150 pound animal).

When bowhunting from a tree stand the tendency is to shoot high. Many times the arrow enters the deer high in the chest cavity and does not exit. When this happens the high entrance hole means trailing may be difficult. If you want to recover an animal hit in this fashion, you must do so within an hour after hitting the buck, before the hole clots shut. Also, if a wounded deer beds, the wound has a greater chance of clotting and closing because the heartbeat of a moving whitetail is three times greater than a bedded one. So, with the exception of a gut-shot deer, I do not wait long before tak-

ing up the track of a deer hit with an arrow. And if it is rain-
ing I take up the track even sooner.

During gun season I take a different approach to following
wounded deer. Bullets kill differently than arrows, by tissue
damage, bleeding, and shock. This, along with gun season's
hunting pressure, causes me to take up the trail quickly.
However, just how quickly is dictated by where I'm gun hunting. If I'm hunting New York's or Pennsylvania's opening day,
where hunting pressure is intense, I trail immediately. If I'm
in the wilds of Saskatchewan, where just the wolves and I are
in the area, I take my time.

Finding The Trail

It's important to mark where you shot from before going to
where you feel the deer was standing when the shot was
taken. Once you find where the deer was, mark the location
with toilet paper. Be careful not to disturb the site, as you
may need to come back to it later. Hair will usually be evident
before blood is found, so look carefully for it. Knowing where

*Shot placement is critical. Whitetails will not travel far if your shot
placement is good.*

different color hair is located on a whitetail's body can go a long way in revealing where it was hit. If mostly brown hair is found, it's an indication of a body hit or a high hit. If it's white, it was a low hit. Also, if there is little hair, it probably means a body shot. A lot of hair is an indication of a grazing shot.

Quietly follow the trail until you find blood, being careful not to walk in the trail of turned up leaves. When you find blood, carefully study it to determine the location of the wound. At this point (under most of my bowhunting conditions) a half hour has passed since I took the shot. It's at this point that a trailing strategy can be determined. As mentioned previously, if you know the deer was hit in a vital area, it's best to get on the trail in order to keep the animal bleeding.

If you're sure of a gut shot, the buck will usually be bedded within five hundred yards of where it was hit. And if jumped, it will have the ability to run for a long time before dropping. As a result I mark the spot where the deer was hit and wait several hours before taking up the trail, providing there are not a lot of hunters in the woods.

The Blood Factor

Some hunters swear that the color and consistency of blood can determine where the deer was hit. Though some hunters are adept at this, most are not. In spite of the fact that many "experts" claim that pink blood means a lung shot, dark blood a liver or paunch shot, and semi-dark blood a heart shot, the difference between blood from these areas is minimal and difficult to identify.

But, there are times that a lung shot can be easily identified by bubbles in bright pink blood. When such blood is found, the trailing process will usually not take long, with death coming within two hundred yards. Bright red blood coming from both sides of the body reveals a good hit and the animal should be recovered in a short period of time. Don't be overly concerned that blood on a sapling or tall weed is from a high hit. Though this could be the case, it's probably because the deer ran over it while escaping.

While lung or heart shot deer are the easiest to follow, a gut shot whitetail presents the toughest trailing challenge. Often a gut-shot deer will bleed well initially. However, it doesn't take long for the blood trail to diminish and end altogether as the wound clots shut. One way to determine a gut shot at the shot site is to look for particles of food or bile. Another is by looking at the consistency of the blood. Gut-shot blood often looks like it's watered down. Also sniff the blood to check for foul smells.

Next to a gut shot deer, the toughest deer to recover is one hit in a muscle, shoulder blade, neck, back, or leg. On the opening day of our gun season last year, my son Aaron shot at and hit a five point whitetail. About fifteen minutes after I heard him shoot, I went to his stand and we took up the trail. The buck had been standing about forty yards from him when he pulled the trigger. Though we found hair at the location, we didn't find blood until we had followed the turned up leaves for thirty yards. At this point there was plenty of blood and the tracking was easy for the first two hundred yards. Then the blood trail began to thin out. We slowly followed the blood trail for another two hundred yards before a shot rang out in front of us. Unfortunately it was opening day of New York's shotgun season and the buck ran into another hunter before we could recover it. Aaron had hit the buck in the front shoulder, forward of the heart area. Though the shot would have been lethal, the hit was classic of a wound in the large muscles. With these types of wounds there are usually large patches of blood soon after the hit, but the blood trail diminishes to spots as the wound begins to clot after two hundred yards. With such hits, tracking becomes a slow process.

Finding The Animal

Despite what some may say, you can't predict a wounded whitetail's behavior. They don't always run downhill, to water, or go in a straight course after they are hit. After the shot it's easy to take off helter-skelter in the direction you think the deer will go. But don't. Suppress this urge and force yourself to follow the sign. Once you start trailing the deer, move quietly but as quickly as possible. Often a wounded deer will allow you to approach closely if you don't make a lot of noise. So, make sure you don't crash through the woods and don't talk loudly if someone is with you. When trailing a wounded deer I do it cautiously, just like when I'm hunting.

When I take up the trail I periodically mark the trail with toilet paper. Some use surveyor's tape but I prefer not to because it's not biodegradable, and I'd have to come back and take it down when I'm finished. If the blood sign is light, mark each speck of blood in order to line up the animal's escape route. Also, make sure you do not walk on the trail because you may need to come back and recheck it later.

If the trail stops abruptly, check the immediate area to make sure the deer didn't backtrack. I've had more than one buck do this over the years. If the trail ends, mark the last speck of blood and begin slowly circling the area. If this isn't fruitful, backtrack to make sure you didn't miss something. Also, check surrounding trails for blood sign. If you are

Stay calm and go slow when tracking. Make sure you mark your blood trail with toilet paper, should you have to backtrack or go for help.

After the animal is harvested it's time to savor the moment and reflect upon the hunt.

unable to find the deer yourself, go for help. On more than one occasion I've contacted friends to search for a wounded whitetail. With the help of many well-trained eyes, the trailing process becomes easier as one person can stay on the trail while the others fan out. Always be aware that a wounded deer may circle and try to go back in the direction it came from. When all else fails, sit down and listen. Often jays, crows, ravens, and magpies will be attracted to a downed deer.

If you come upon a wounded animal and it's standing or bedded with its head up, be prepared to shoot again. Also, approach a downed deer slowly and quietly from behind, being alert for signs of life. If it doesn't move, jab it with a stick, arrow, or the barrel of your gun. If it moves, kill it with an arrow to the chest cavity or a gunshot to the neck.

10 TRAILING TIPS TO REMEMBER

1. Stay calm after the shot and try to determine shot placement.
2. Wait fifteen to twenty minutes before pursuing.

3. Mark where you shot from.
4. Mark where the deer was standing when shot.
5. Check for hair.
6. Find blood before actually trailing.
7. Try to determine where the deer was hit. If it's a muscle or vital area hit, pursue immediately. If it's a gut shot, wait.
8. Proceed slowly and quietly. Constantly look ahead.
9. Mark trail with toilet paper.
10. Make sure deer is dead before approaching.

HOW HEAVY IS THAT DEER?

In the past, determining the weight of a whitetail in the field was nearly impossible. Now with the aid of the following chart, developed by Virginia Polytechnic Institute & State University, this process has been simplified. To calculate live or hog-dressed weight, first measure heart girth, the circumference of the body just behind the front legs. Then consult the chart to convert girth into a close estimate of weight.

	Hog-dressed weight	Live weight
Heart girth inches (cm)	**Adults pounds (kg)**	**Adults pounds (kg)**
26 (66.0)	46 (20.9)	60 (27.2)
27 (68.6)	52 (23.6)	68 (30.8)
28 (71.1)	58 (26.3)	75 (34.0)
29 (73.7)	64 (29.0)	83 (37.6)
30 (76.2)	70 (31.8)	90 (40.8)
31 (78.7)	76 (34.5)	98 (44.5)
32 (81.3)	82 (37.2)	106 (48.1)
33 (83.8)	88 (39.9)	113 (51.3)
34 (86.4)	94 (42.6)	121 (54.9)
35 (88.9)	101 (45.8)	128 (58.1)
36 (91.4)	107 (48.5)	136 (61.7)
37 (94.0)	113 (51.3)	144 (65.3)
38 (96.5)	119 (54.0)	151 (68.5)

Heart girth inches (cm)	Hog-dressed weight Adults pounds (kg)	Live weight Adults pounds (kg)
39 (99.1)	125 (56.7)	159 (72.1)
40 (101.6)	131 (59.2)	166 (75.3)
41 (104.1)	137 (62.1)	174 (78.9)
42 (106.7)	143 (64.9)	182 (82.6)
43 (109.2)	149 (67.6)	190 (86.2)
44 (111.8)	155 (70.3)	197 (89.4)
45 (114.3)	161 (73.0)	205 (93.0)

Virginia Polytechnic Institute & State University

chapter 13

TOOLS OF THE GAME

From an equipment standpoint I'm a firm believer in the idea that form follows function. This is not to say that I don't have nice equipment, because I do. When I returned from Vietnam in 1970 one of the first things I purchased was a beautiful Weatherby Mark V rifle. Though it looked great in the gun cabinet, it was less than functional in the field because of its high gloss finish. To remedy this I had the metal surfaces matte-blued and the stock refinished in an oil finish. This toned down the glare, making the rifle far more practical in hunting situations. Over the years I've worked hard at trying to make all of my hunting gear more practical for the field. It hasn't always been easy to do this, but in most cases I've succeeded.

GUNS

Though I own a beautiful Winchester Model 94 in 30-30 caliber, I long ago stopped deer hunting with calibers such as the 30-30 and the .35 Remington. I fully realize that both are legendary deer calibers. However, in my opinion these and calibers like them are marginal deer rounds when compared with calibers such as the .270, .280, .308, and .30-06. To adequately and consistently kill a whitetail, it's generally felt that a bullet should have at least 1,200 foot pounds of energy at impact to get the job done. Calibers such as the .30-30 are marginal in this regard. So with this in mind, bullet weight and velocity are important factors to consider.

I've been in a lot of deer camps over the years and the most popular whitetail calibers have been the .270, .280, 7mm Rem-

A model 7600 Remington .30-06 is my big woods Eastern deer rifle. It's lightweight and fast handling.

ington Mag., .308, and .30-06. These are the choices of serious whitetail hunters. When loaded with the proper bullets, they are lethal from 30 to 300 yards and beyond, and more than enough for even the biggest whitetails roaming the continent. Though I've seen a fair number of 300 magnums sitting in camp gun racks, they are simply too much gun for a white-tailed buck and the hunter pulling the trigger. The problem with using magnums for whitetail hunting is that excessive muzzle blast and recoil overwhelms the average deer hunter and causes poor shot placement due to flinching.

I've rifle hunted whitetails with everything from a .243 to belted magnums, but my favorite calibers are the .270 and .30-06. I guess this is partly because I was a big Jack O'Connor fan growing up. It's also due to the job I've seen each do on trophy class bucks. I use rifles suited for the terrain I'm hunting. If I'm hunting dense forests such as New York's Adirondack Mountains, I use a modified Remington 7600 slide action .30-06. The rifle was reworked by Harold Torre of The Whitetail Gun Shop in Essex Junction, Vermont (802-878-7133). These folks specialize in reducing the weight of slide action Remington rifles by remilling the barrels and removing wood from the buttstock. My scoped 7600 handles like a dream and weighs less than seven pounds loaded. It's just the ticket for big woods whitetail hunting. Several of my other whitetail rifles have been worked on by

Tom Fargnoli of Naples, New York (716-374-2814), who specializes in building custom deer and elk rifles.

When I hunt in country that offers shots out to 300 yards and beyond, I use either a .257 Weatherby Magnum or a .270, both of which are equipped with synthetic stocks. Though it isn't the nicest looking gun I have, the .270 Model 700 Remington bolt action is my pride and joy. It fits me perfectly and the 130 Nosler Ballistic Tip bullets (pushed by 55 grains of IMR 4350 powder) I hand load are extremely accurate and lethal on whitetails. In spite of the recent advancements in factory ammunition, I hand load for all my rifles, including the .30-30. I push the .257 Weatherby's 100 grain bullets with 64 grains of IMR 4350 powder. With a muzzle velocity of over 3,500 feet per second, this load is excellent for open country whitetail hunting. The load I use in the two .30-06's I own is 165 grain bullets pushed by 57 grains of IMR 4350. This load exceeds 2,800 feet per second and is an excellent whitetail load out to 300 yards. After years of use I feel the 165 grain bullet is the best all around .30-06 load and an excellent choice when bigger animals such as bear and moose can also be hunted.

I'm not a long distance shooter, and would not think of shooting at a buck over 300 yards away, unless conditions were perfect. Deer hunting is not woodchuck hunting and prone shooting is seldom possible in the deer woods. For this reason I sight in my rifles to hit an inch-and-one-half to two inches high

One piece of equipment I use a lot in the deer woods is a BackSeat, which is a combination day pack and seat. It's just the ticket for hunters who like to sit.

Slug guns have come a long way in the last ten years. The one I currently use is nearly as accurate as a rifle to 75 yards.

If I had to limit myself to three weapons for whitetail hunting, it would be my Remington slug gun, synthetic stocked .270, and compound bow. I use these more than any equipment I own.

at 100 yards (it depends on caliber), which makes them dead on at about 200 yards. By sighting in for 200 yards my loads are dead on at 50 yards, an inch high at 175 yards, and approximately six inches low at 300 yards. I sight in for 200 instead of 300 yards because I've hunted whitetails across North America and the average distance of all my rifle kills has been 115 yards. Frankly I've never attempted a shot further than 225 yards as I feel it's too risky under normal hunting conditions.

Fortunately it hasn't happened to me, but I've witnessed some real horror stories with damaged rifles on deer hunts. On more than one occasion I've seen a hunter's rifle stock break or scopes malfunction. For this reason I always carry two rifles when hunting away from home. Murphy with his infamous Murphy's Law seems to always be in the camp I'm in. It never fails. So, I prepare for the worst and hope for the best.

I cut my whitetail teeth hunting with shotguns and rifled slugs. While growing up on the farm I loved to hunt woodchucks with my .222 and .243. Then, when deer season rolled around I'd get depressed because I had to switch to a slug gun. In my formative years I viewed this as a real downer because few shotguns were accurate shooting Foster style slugs. But, no more.

In the last five years slug gun technology has taken a quantum leap. Manufacturers, realizing there are more slug gun hunters than rifle hunters (because of game laws), have rushed to provide more accurate slugs and guns. I currently use a Remington 11/87 deer gun, equipped with a Hastings rifled slug barrel and a 2X7 power Leupold shotgun scope. This particular gun has no problem grouping three slugs into a two-and-one-half inch hole at seventy yards, which is the distance I zero in my slug guns for. I also occasionally use a Mossburg Model 835 that, like the Remington, groups most sabot slugs very well. Also the 11/87 shoots Winchester's Foster style slugs nearly as well as sabots, which is an added bonus because Foster style slugs are less expensive than sabots. So, with this kind of accuracy I no longer feel handicapped when New York's gun season arrives.

Because shotgun hunting involves foul weather and close quarter encounters with whitetails, my 11/87 is equipped with a synthetic stock and matte finish. The Mossburg 12 gauge has a Realtree finish on a synthetic stock.

In order to make my deer rifles more functional during inclement weather, I do a few extra things. Even though most synthetic stock manufacturers say their stocks don't need extra work, I've had all of my synthetic stocked rifles' actions bedded and the barrels floated by a gunsmith. This improves accuracy immensely. In addition I have all my rifles' triggers adjusted to a three pound trigger pull. This has given me more confidence and made me a much more accurate shooter. And lastly, rifle hunting for whitetails often means cold weather snow hunting (especially in Canada). Because of this more than one hunter has lost a chance at a trophy of a lifetime when a firing pin froze up. For this reason I have all my rifles' triggers and bolts degreased so they will not freeze up in cold weather.

The most important rifle in my arsenal is a .22 Ruger Model 77/22 equipped with a Leupold .22 four power scope. This gun's importance might seem odd but it's the gun I stay sharp with. As deer season approaches I take a few minutes each day (rain or shine) to shoot twenty rounds off hand at a flipper target from a distance of 25 yards. The target has three different size metal circles and when I can consistently hit the three-quarter-inch circle my confidence soars. This gun, with its three pound trigger pull and big game style scope, allows me to fine tune my shooting skills so I'm the best shot I can be by the time the season rolls around. Getting in my daily rounds with the .22 is just as important as daily archery practice prior to bow season.

ARCHERY

Though I grew up with rifles and very much enjoy shooting them, my first love is archery hunting. Simply put, the challenge of hunting whitetails at close quarters with a bow and arrow is what whitetail hunting is all about. To get a white-tailed buck within twenty yards is no easy task and requires that the hunter and equipment be one. Because I strive to

When it comes to bow and arrows I prefer a wheel compound (sixty pound pull) and aluminum arrows.

become better each season, my choice of archery tackle has changed over the years.

My first bow was a simple forty-five-pound fiberglass recurve. After one fall with it I moved to a Bear recurve and found that I could shoot considerably better. However, it wasn't until I started using a compound that my proficiency increased to where I was consistently killing deer with arrows.

From the standpoint of what is available on the market, my preferences in archery tackle could be construed as pretty basic. Though I occasionally shoot with a release, I do all of my serious deer hunting with fingers (tab or glove). I currently shoot a top-of-the-line Golden Eagle sixty-pound compound equipped with two sight pins. One is set for ten yards and the other for twenty yards. I prefer a wheel compound to a cam because a wheel bow is quieter and easier for me to shoot.

I do not shoot with an overdraw. Currently I'm shooting 31-inch 2216 aluminum arrows topped with 125 grain Satellite Titan heads. This four blade broadhead not only has a large cutting surface but also flies the same as 125 grain target points.

In spite of all the hype and advertising, most bows are pretty much the same when it comes to quality. However, the sound they make when shot is not always the same. A key in successful whitetail hunting is how quiet a bow is when the moment of truth arrives. Whenever I get my hands on a hunting bow I go over it to see where the noises are. After pulling it back a few

A bow can be made quieter by equipping it with a Townsend speed slide, gluing leather to the arrow rest, and adding catwhisker silencers to the bow string.

times and then shooting it, I'm able to determine if there are any noises in the bow's eccentrics. Often, when pulled to full draw, a wheel will squeak. To eliminate the sound I apply unscented Pledge or vegetable oil to the wheel axle or string channel. Some people suggest using a light lubricant such as WD-40. However, I shy away from any petroleum-based lubricant because of its odor.

After silencing the bow's eccentrics I go to work on the arrow rest. Having a silent arrow rest is critical when it comes time to draw on a buck. I cut a piece of rawhide and glue it below and above the arrow rest so that if the arrow falls off the rest it does not hit any metal surface. When it comes to the actual arrow rest there are a number of ways to go. Though metal spring rests are popular with 3-D shooters, I stay away from any metal rest as nothing is louder than the sound of metal to metal coming together. I keep things simple and use a rest compatible with aluminum and carbon arrows. In other words the rest must be dead silent when I pull the arrow back.

Once the arrow rest is taken care of, it's important to make sure the cable guard slide performs in both wet and dry conditions. Most bow manufacturers skimp when it comes to cable guard slides, so it's important to find one that is quiet in all weather conditions. There are several aftermarket slides available and I've had great success using a Townsend speed slide on my bows. If you want to go with the slide that came on your bow, it can be made to slide quietly by spraying silicone on the cable guard to eliminate friction. Also, if you get in a pinch, wipe facial oil off your nose with your fingers and rub this oil on the cable guard. It works quite well.

If precautions are not taken, a lot of noise can be created when an arrow is released from a bow. Due to the shape of cams, the string almost always slaps when an arrow is released, thereby making more noise than wheels. For this reason wheel bows are quieter, which is one of the reasons I shoot a wheel bow. I use two rubber cat whisker silencers to quiet the string. Avoid using fabric puff silencers because they take on moisture when it rains and the added weight slows arrow flight up to five feet per second. Should noise in the bow persist, I opt for a bow stabilizer.

The last step in a bow's noise creation comes when the arrow clears the bow. When this happens vibration is at its peak. To eliminate as much noise as possible, I tighten most screws on the bow and quiver with Loc-Tite to make sure they stay tight no matter how much I shoot. I also make sure the arrows in my quiver are aligned in such a way that the feathers or vanes are not touching. If they do touch, they will rub together during the release, causing unwanted noise.

Though I hunt with arrows fletched with both vanes and feathers, I prefer feathers. To waterproof feathers and make them perform better, spray them with unscented hair spray.

This keeps them from picking up moisture and adding weight to the arrow.

STANDS

When I first began deer hunting nearly all of my stand hunting was from permanent wood stands that I built. As I became a better hunter, I realized that permanent stands limited the way I could hunt whitetails, especially mature bucks. For added mobility I purchased my first portable stand (a Baker climber) in the early 1980s. I immediately fell in love with the concept of using a portable stand to put me where the action was hot.

Though I own and occasionally use climbing stands, I shy away from them because they're noisy. A mature buck is cagey and the least little foreign noise will send him into orbit, so I'm noise conscious when I hunt. For this reason I rely on lock-on style stands for the bulk of my hunting. Also, lock-on stands are strong. Though lock-ons have been my stand of choice for the past ten years, I'm starting to use more ladder type stands. Why? Because I'm getting older and safety is an increasing consideration.

When I first began using portable stands, weight was a big factor in considering which stand to use. No more! Today most manufacturers use lightweight aluminum that is strong. The light weight of aluminum stands also allows them to be hung easily. For this reason I choose aluminum over steel stands.

A key feature I look for in a portable stand is platform size. In a cold climate, where I'm typically standing for long periods of time, I insist on a stand with a large platform. Cold temperatures require that you stand a lot in order to stay warm. I do toe raises and all kinds of minimal-movement exercises to keep warm in a stand. The reality of it all is that after three hours in sub-freezing temperatures, one's body starts to do unusual things. Reaction time and eye focus begins to slow. Hand flexibility diminishes. In all, the prospect of losing one's balance is very real. Therefore, it is important to have as big a platform as possible. I look for a platform with at least 576 square inches (24x24 inches) of surface area.

In addition to platform size, make sure the stand's seat can be folded up when you stand up, otherwise the seat will continually cut into the back of your legs. Also, I like a seat that is higher than the normal 17-inch seat height. By having a seat at least 20 inches high, you'll be in better position when a buck shows up. And lastly I continually look for a better safety belt. As a result I seem to be using a different one each year to ensure my safety when hunting above the ground.

Proper clothing can make or break a hunter in the woods. By knowing how to layer, most conditions can be conquered.

CLOTHING

Down through the years I've hunted in about every kind of clothing imaginable, from blue jeans to cotton work coveralls to wool. During the last few years I've discovered that none of my early hunting garments can stack up to what's available today. Probably the greatest advances in hunting (aside from the compound bow) have been in the area of clothing. When I began deer hunting in the sixties, wool was the ticket. But wool became heavy when wet, and trying to dry it was often impossible in a hunting camp. Today synthetics abound and the hunter has an array of clothing options to choose from.

The key to handling deer season's endurance test is dressing right for the occasion. I have several different patterns of camouflage I like to wear during bow season. None of it is waterproof. In order to stay dry and warm, I purchase it large enough to wear over waterproof and warm clothing.

It may seem simplistic but layering is the key to beating inclement weather conditions. The secret to layering your clothing is to trap air between the layers of garments, thereby insulating your body. To keep from perspiring I never head for a stand with all my clothing on my back. Rather, I have a fleece backpack that contains the bulk of the clothing I intend to wear. If I'm bowhunting from a stand, I stop and put on the required clothing when I'm a couple hundred yards from the stand.

Temperature, moisture, and the length of time I intend to sit dictate what I will wear. On cool damp days I wear polypropylene underwear that wicks the moisture away from my body. Polypropylene is an amazing fabric that enables a person to stay dry and warm longer. Generally it comes in three weights: light, medium, and heavyweight. To eliminate bulk I recommend the medium weight polypropylene for general hunting purposes.

Beating the rain often requires good rain gear. As mentioned previously, wool picks up weight in rain. Down clothing is warm and lightweight but worthless once it gets wet. In attempts to come up with a lighter garment many hunters have turned to Gore-Tex to stay dry. The beauty of Gore-Tex is that it is able to breathe so that moisture doesn't build up in the undergarments. When first introduced Gore-Tex was noisy. Now many manufacturers have taken the noise out of Gore-Tex hunting gear by covering it with fleece or wool, allowing the hunter to be quiet in the woods.

During bow season when the temperatures range from 32 to 60 degrees, I layer my clothing to allow for a four-hour sit. If it's in the thirties I'll wear polypropylene underwear and fleece garments under my camouflage. I also recommend a nylon or polypropylene inner sock and a wool outer sock. The inner sock wicks perspiration away from the foot to the outer sock, allowing one's feet to stay warm and dry.

Well over 50 percent of heat loss is through your head. Therefore, I go to great pains to make sure my head is well-covered and warm. My favorite hat for hunting in the rain and snow is a watch cap made of polypropylene and Gore-Tex. It not only keeps my head warm but also dry. They come in various camo patterns and are marketed by the larger catalog outfitters.

Nothing forces a hunter out of the woods faster than cold feet, so keeping the toes warm is a must. During bow season I often wear knee-high rubber boots to hide human odor...a carryover from my trapping days. The boots are big enough to slip over my lightweight hunting boots. The socks, hunting boots, and rubber boots work as an excellent layering system and are more than enough to keep my feet warm.

If I'm hunting in extreme cold, I layer my clothing to the hilt. Here's an example of how I dress when hunting in Canada, where the temperatures are often around zero. First I put on lightweight polypropylene underwear. Over this I put on a heavyweight layer of polypropylene underwear. Next I put on a heavy wool shirt (Maine Guide Shirt, sold by L.L. Bean) and a pair of sweatpants. Over this I wear a "dry plus Thinsulate" Cabela's Super Slam camouflage fleece suit. In my pack I carry a fleece warm-up jacket should I need extra warmth. On my feet

Proper clothing can make or break a hunter in the woods. By knowing how to layer, most conditions can be conquered.

I wear polypropylene socks next to my skin and a pair of heavy thermal or wool socks over them. My boots are L.L. Bean cold weather packs with wool liners. I also make sure that I have extra dry liners so I can put a dry set in the boots each day. Though I carry disposable air-activated hand and body warmers, I use them only on rare occasions.

From an equipment standpoint I rely heavily on three other things. First, when gun hunting from stands in cold weather I use a sleeping bag. Actually it's a bag I've modified for deer hunting and is just the ticket for staying warm in temperatures below 35 degrees. I've been using this technique for a few years and in the last two years have killed seven whitetails while sitting in the cozy confines of the bag.

Over the last few years I've refined the way I use a bag to make it more efficient and less awkward. It's critical that a sleeping bag be quiet when used for hunting. As a result an inexpensive cotton bag is the best. Because most cotton-lined bags have a nylon outer shell, I advise hunters to turn the bag inside out so the cotton inner liner is on the outside. Doing this keeps things quiet, should the bag rub on the stand platform or the edge of the stand.

If you want to modify the bag you can do a couple of things to make the concept even better. I've purchased fleece material and had an upholsterer sew the fleece on the nylon side of the bag. Doing this makes the bag super quiet on both sides so that I can keep the cotton side inside the bag where it belongs. Also I have two two-inch elastic bands sewn on the open end of the bag so they can go over my shoulders (like suspenders) after I get into the bag. This keeps the bag from falling down.

Lastly I have a sixteen-inch slit sewn into the non-zippered side of the bag. The slit allows me to get my arm out of the bag quickly when something shows up. The other side of the bag has the zipper so a slit isn't needed. By sliding into the bag (with all my clothes and boots on) and pulling it up to my shoulders, I'm able to stay warm as toast in temperatures near zero. It is the ultimate in layering.

Based on experience there are two cautionary notes that need to be stressed when using a sleeping bag. First, if you are hunting from a tree stand, a good safety belt must be used. When you are in a sleeping bag, mobility is limited and it is easy to lose your balance if you aren't careful. Secondly, because of the bag's bulkiness, this technique is not well suited to bowhunting unless the bag comes no higher than your waist. To keep the bag from taking on a mildew smell, I open it up and hang it to dry each night. Once you try a bag you'll undoubtedly ask the same question I did: "Why didn't I do this before?"

Because of the amount of equipment I carry (camera, small tripod, drag rope, etc.) I use a small specialized day pack. The pack I use is called a BackSeat and is tailor-made for my needs.

The fruits of a sleeping bag hunt. During the last two years I've killed five northern whitetails while hunting from a bag. Nothing beats it.

Not only is it compact but it also has a collapsible seat that doubles as a packframe.

One of the last things I want to mention is the cover-up scent I use. In order to consistently kill whitetails you have to beat their noses. Let's face it, in spite of all the best laid plans wind currents often change, so controlling body odors, keeping clothing clean, and using a good cover-up is essential. Though there are many good ones on the market, I've been using Essence of Fall since it came out and am amazed by how well it works. I spray it on all my gear to kill human odor and it works great on the sleeping bag, keeping it free from mildew odor. It's a part of all my hunts.

Because a person exhales over 250 liters of breath into the air each hour I go out of my way to cover up mouth odor. There are two ways a hunter can keep a whitetail from detecting breath odors. One way is to chew a chlorophyll gum, like Golden Eagle Archery's Breath Away gum. The other way is to carry an apple in your pocket and periodically break a chunk of it off and suck on it while on stand. Apples are known as "nature's toothbrush" and take away bad breath.

chapter 14

HUNTING WITH A CAMERA

As I write this chapter, dew is heavy on the wildflowers. It's late summer and deer season is nearly two months away. This morning I spent the better part of two hours in a field of wild-flowers trying to "bag" the right pose of a touch-me-not flower. It was exhilarating. In spite of the fact that I'm from a farm background, love athletics, and chase whitetails throughout the year, I'm addicted to nature photography. I'm told I'm a bit of an enigma to the "leaf lover" crowd who find it hard to believe that I can pursue and capture nature's majesty on film and also take up a bow or gun and hunt wild animals. Though this might be perplexing to some, it's not to me.

When I was growing up on the farm I learned to love all of nature. From my earliest recollection it was evident that God created this beautiful universe for us to enjoy. It was also evident that God put us here as His stewards to take care of the earth. With this as a foundation I came to understand the balance of nature and the part man plays in molding and managing its resources. I was a teenager when I came to the conclusion that wild animal populations had to be controlled in order for them to be healthy and thrive. Also, my farm upbringing taught me that killing is not some evil act, as so many in the animal rights movement view it.

Yes, those early days on the farm taught me to deeply appreciate God's creation. During those formative years I also fell in love with hunting. In 1969 I found myself in Vietnam with the United States Air Force. While there I discovered photography. Little did I know that it would reshape my life. In December of 1970 I returned to the United States with a 35mm camera and a couple of telephoto lenses. In January I went back to college and began photographing whitetails in a wintering area close to the school I attended. I spent that winter hitting the books and photographing whitetails. This experience hooked me on hunting with a camera.

After graduating from college I took a sales and marketing position with a large corporation. I enjoyed the job very much and figured I'd do it the rest of my life. However, all this time I continued to hunt more and more with a camera and shot everything from wildflowers to whitetails with film. I also began dabbling in writing and selling photos. In September of 1979 an opportunity came along and I jumped into the nature photography/outdoor writing field full time. At the time it seemed like a scary move but I never looked back. With a wonderful wife and son to support me, my photography improved with each passing year. The last fifteen years have truly been a blessing.

Unfortunately photographing nature involves much more than merely picking up a camera, loading it with film, and shooting random photos. It takes knowledge, practice, and what I view as a gift, to compete with the best. However, this chapter is not meant to turn you into a professional photographer. My intention is to provide a few tips to help you become a hunter with a camera and allow you to better record your hunting experience.

As I discovered in January of 1970, the beauty of hunting deer with a camera is that the season lasts all year and there are no bag limits. The battery of "camera guns" I used to take the photos in this book are shown here. I shoot Nikon cameras and lenses and presently rely heavily on three lenses: a 35-70mm f2.8 zoom, an 80-200mm f2.8 ED zoom and a 200-400 f4 ED zoom. These lenses are extremely sharp (and expensive!) and

One of the goals of a nature photographer is to sell his images. Here are some of the magazine covers I've been fortunate to sell over the years.

To take great photos requires good equipment. Nearly all of the photos in this book were taken with these cameras.

allow me to photograph when the light is less than adequate. I always try to use the 80-200 zoom mounted on a tripod or camera gun-stock, though I sometimes shoot it offhand if lighting permits. The 200-400 zoom is heavy and is always used with a tripod, to ensure that the pictures are as sharp as possible.

The color film I use changes with technology. Presently I use four color slide films: Fuji Velvia (ASA 50) for scenics, Kodachrome 64 (ASA 64) and Kodak Lumiere 100X (ASA 100) for animals and hunter setups, and Kodachrome 200 for dim light situations. You might ask, why so many films? Well, keep in mind that I do this professionally, and the competition is keen, so I try to find the best film for the occasion. The reason I currently use Fuji Velvia for scenics is that it is one of the sharpest films made and its colors are incredible. Kodachrome 64 is my workhorse film, is very sharp, and renders fur colors accurately. This is my "whitetail film." Kodak Lumiere is a sharp film with a little more speed than Kodachrome 64 and its colors are nearly as good as Velvia. It's a great all-around film for scenics, animals, and for hunter setups because its speed (ASA 100) allows me to shoot with less light than Velvia or Kodachrome 64. And lastly, I shoot Kodachrome 200 when I'm out of light and need to get the photo. Though it is a sharp film, it does not give good colors, which is common of fast speed film.

As far as film is concerned, remember a couple of things. First, always shoot slide film. In most cases better prints can be made from slides than with print film and you'll have the slides for projection purposes, and if you are fortunate, for possible magazine sales. Second, the slower ASA film will be sharper and have better colors. Unfortunately everything is a trade-off and using slow speed film usually means shooting off a tripod.

EQUIPMENT

Whenever someone asks me about what camera I'd recommend for photographing whitetails, I ask them how much money they are willing to spend. Today's cameras are not cheap and the more "bells and whistles" they have, the more costly they are. For the novice to serious amateur I recommend a medium priced 35mm camera body (with a good self-timer built in) and a zoom lens in the 35-70mm range. This lens has a magnification of wide angle to about one and one-quarter power and is excellent for scenics and hunter setup photos (note that a lens' magnification can be calculated by dividing 50 into the lens' millimeter). Most of today's medium priced camera bodies are as good as the top-of-the-line models of ten years ago and have excellent light meters and often auto-focus features. They also have built-in autowinders, which many refer to as motor drives. These can be good and bad. The good side is that the winder automatically advances the film so you can get to the next frame before the action changes. The bad side is the noise they make. Winder noise is foreign to whitetails and often spooks them. So, try to find a camera with a quiet autowinder.

In order to get started photographing deer a zoom lens in the 80-200mm range is essential. Also, it's best to get one with the lowest "f" setting you can afford. I have two 80-200 lenses that are f2.8s and they allow me to photograph in dim light (the smaller the "f" number the less light required to take a picture). People often think most deer photos are taken with long lenses. Though many are, the 80-200 is my workhorse lens and the bulk of my photos are taken with the 80-200 rather than the real long lenses.

For the person serious about photographing whitetails a 300mm, or better yet, a 400mm is a must for photographing the hard to approach animals. A 300mm (6 power) and 400mm (8 power) allow you to bring the animal in close without spooking it. In most instances the deer photographs that grace the covers of major magazines are taken with 300, 400, or 500mm lenses. The downside of these lenses are their weight and cost. The weight of most requires the use of a tripod. And the sticker price on these lenses can make a person cry or tremble, depending on his or her frame of mind. At today's prices one can expect to pay anywhere from $500 for a long telephoto to over $4,000 for a top-of-the-line model. As with the other lenses, the lower the "f" setting the better your chances of photography in dim light. The lower "f" setting lenses will also be the most expensive.

Though it isn't necessary, a good portable blind is nice to have. I've used this Rue blind often over the years with great success.

A sturdy tripod is one of the last pieces of equipment required to get into deer photography. Even though it's the last piece of equipment I mention, don't try to skimp on price as the quality of your photos will be in direct proportion to how steady the camera is when the photo is taken. My lightweight tripod, the one I use for most of my hunter setups, is a Gitzo 226 with a Slik Pro ball head. It's compact and sturdy for its size and goes with me wherever I hunt. The tripod I use for my long lenses is a Gitzo 320 with an ARCA ball head. This tripod is sturdy...and heavy.

One piece of equipment that isn't necessary but nice to have for whitetail photography is a portable blind. You can either make your own or purchase one of the many on the market. Dollar for dollar Leonard Lee Rue's Ultimate Blind is hard to beat. Rue's blind is lightweight and can be put in place in less than a minute. I've spent many hours in this blind and have taken some great photos with it. (This blind can be purchased by calling Rue Enterprises at 800-734-2568.)

TAKING THE PHOTO

When I first began photographing whitetails I didn't have a clue as to what I was doing and had to learn as I went. During

One way to enhance wildlife photos is to add scenery to the photo. In this case I wanted to show not only the Dall sheep but also the country they live in.

In photography the eyes are the center of attention. Therefore, always try to focus on an animal's eyes when taking a photo.

those first few years I was more intent to just get the deer in the frame than thinking about composition, depth of field, or lighting. All these aspects of photography take time to develop but with a little knowledge the learning curve can be shortened.

When composing a deer or hunter photo I try to think how the subject will look best in the picture. As a result I often put the subject off center in the picture so it becomes a part of the scene. In order to enhance the photo's composition I'll try to find a tree or some other object to frame the person or animal with. From an

Backlighting photos can be tricky but with a little practice you'll be able to capture the mood of the moment.

artistic standpoint these things make the photos much better. To put it another way I prefer to have my photos tell a story. This is not to say that I don't take tight portraits, because I do, but when the opportunity presents itself I try to get artistic. An example of what I mean can be illustrated by the Dall Sheep (page 196) that I photographed in Alaska. Though I have many tight portraits of sheep, this photo tells much more about the sheep and the country they live in. To get the sheep and the background in sharp focus I set the "f" setting to f8 on the lens. Usually at f8 or higher the foreground, subject, and background will be in focus. This is a tip you'll want to remember.

Whenever I take portraits of people or animals I focus on their eyes. The eye is the center of attention and reveals the soul and character of the subject. Also, the glint of the eye adds to the overall photo. In addition I like to take these photos from the subject's eye level. If it's a fawn lying on the forest

floor it means photographing from your belly like the fawn photo shows (page 196).

Light is the key to photography and when possible I try to position the animal or hunter so they will not be in direct sunlight. If I have a choice I'll opt to photograph the subject in cross or back light whenever possible. This kind of lighting makes for more dramatic photos, as the accompanying bowhunter and whitetail photos on page 197 illustrate.

But perhaps the greatest challenge in nature photography is capturing the action. Things happen fast in the wild and getting it right doesn't just happen. In order to stop action you need to shoot a shutter speed of at least a 500th of a second, or 1,000th of a second if you have enough light. Of course there will be times when you want to show action by blurring the motion.

The two ruffled grouse photos illustrate two ways to handle action. In the first photo I wanted to stop the wing beats as the grouse drummed. I accomplished this by doing two things. First,

These two photos show what can happen when motion is stopped and allowed to flow. The grouse on the left was shot with a higher shutter speed, to stop the wing beats. The one on the right was shot with a slow shutter speed. This allowed the wings to be blurred so that motion could be seen in the picture.

I knew (from prior photography) that a grouse pauses slightly in its drum roll so in the first photo I waited for this to happen. Second, I increased the shutter speed as much as the available light would allow, which in this case was 125th of a second. By doing these two things I was able to stop the wings in mid motion.

In the second grouse photo I wanted to show the motion of the wing beats so I slowed the shutter speed to a 60th of a second and took the photo when the grouse was in the middle of his drum roll. Both of these photos have won national photo contests and illustrate different ways to capture action.

Handling whitetail action is much different than the action of a grouse. Unlike the grouse photos, where I was able to photograph out of a blind, the next two whitetail photos were taken in the open. The photo of the buck jumping the deadfall was possible because I anticipated the action. This photo was taken when I had two friends drive a small woodlot for me. I positioned myself behind a large oak tree and waited for the action to unfold. Not

Sometimes a photographer needs to be a little lucky. Had a doe not been running ahead of this buck, the photo would not have been possible.

Slowing the shutter speed allowed me to blur the snowflakes in this whitetail photo. In the process I was able to add to the mood of the photo.

long after they entered the woodlot, a doe came bounding right at me and jumped the deadfall. Though I did not take a photo of her I did get my bearings by focusing on her as she jumped. Fifty yards behind her was this buck. Because I was already focused on where the doe jumped, I was ready and took four frames through my motordriven camera (Kodachrome 64 film, 500th of a second, lens at f2.8) when he jumped the deadfall. Two of the four photos came out sharp. In the other deer photo I wanted to depict snow falling. I accomplished this by setting my shutter speed dial to a 60th of a second in order to show motion in the flakes. Had I used any faster shutter speed, like 125th of a second, the snow would not have blurred as I wanted it to.

WHERE TO PHOTOGRAPH WHITETAILS

Photographing whitetails can be done anyplace they are found. Though I do a great deal of whitetail photography on our farm, my best photos come from areas where hunting is limited or prohibited. Many photographers photograph in deer pens, which are found throughout the United States. Though I've occasionally done this, my photos have not been that good

A real bonus of whitetail photography is the other wildlife that happens by when I'm in the woods. I love to photograph wild turkeys and do it often.

because deer found in the confines of small enclosures are usually not photogenic. My best whitetail photography has come from photographing on estates, in national parks (where deer are used to people), and around metropolitan areas where hunting is limited. Nearly every major city in the Northeast has areas where deer have become used to people and are approachable.

There are three keys to getting photos in these areas. First, you need to be prepared to photograph out of a blind where deer are skittish. Second, realize that deer will come to food. If this is legal where you want to photograph (many places it isn't), it's an excellent way to get a whitetail in the position you want. They have a real craving for shelled corn and I've used it throughout the United States as deer photography bait. The last key to deer photography is time. Deer have no watch to go by and move as they please. So, to be successful one must take the time needed to get the photos. In many areas (with the exception of baiting) I hunt whitetail with the camera much the same way I do with bow or gun: from tree stands, off the ground, or by still-hunting.

HUNTER SETUP

Photographing whitetails and other animals is what nature photography is all about. But from a hunting standpoint capturing the hunting experience on film is something I love to do because it allows me to relive the moment.

There's no question that one of the most overlooked aspects of capturing the hunting experience on film is that of taking photos of kill scenes in a way that doesn't offend people. Showing a lot of blood or deer with their tongues hanging out is repulsive to many people, especially the nonhunter, and leaves a poor image of deer hunting. So, photographing this aspect of the hunt is critical to making a good impression.

Nearly all of my hunter setup photos are taken with a 35-70mm Nikon f2.8 lens and an 8008 Nikon body attached to a Gitzo 226 tripod. This camera's self timer is capable of being programmed to allow from one to thirty seconds between the time the shutter is released and the photo is taken. It's a great feature for someone who hunts alone and wishes to take his own photo.

If I'm hunting alone and need to take my own photo, the process is easy. First I program the camera for the amount of time I feel I'll need between the time I press the shutter to the time the photo is taken. Then I compose the photo, press the shutter and move to the predetermined spot where I'll appear in the photo.

Angles can mean everything when photographing a hunter walking up on a deer. After the kill I position the deer where I think it looks best, making sure to take advantage of any nice framing possibilities. Then I usually position the camera a short distance from the buck's head, compose the photo, and focus on the buck's eyes. If I want the hunter to be in sharp focus I make sure that the lens' "f" setting is at least at f8 or higher. If I want the hunter to be slightly out of focus I'll set the "f" setting from f2.8 to f5.6. In the photo of me walking up on a buck I wanted to have both the buck and me be in focus, so I set the lens' "f" setting at f8.

If I'm taking a hero shot, either of myself or someone else, I make sure there is no blood on the deer. Also, I work the angles trying to get the best possible pose. If I'm photographing another hunter with his deer I make sure I'm focused on the deer's eyes if it's a fresh kill. If I'm doing my own self-portrait, things are a little more difficult. To get my own picture I check the scene carefully, noting how high certain branches are around the buck. With this in mind I compose the photo by looking at the branches as a frame of reference so I don't cut my head off in the picture. I then use as high an "f" setting as possible, f8 to f16, so I have a good depth of field (meaning everything is sharp) and take my own portrait. This takes a little getting used to but with practice becomes rather easy.

It's important to make sure that the buck looks like it's a fresh kill. Once a buck has been dead for several hours its eyes glaze and start to become sunken. This problem can be remedied by using a pair of glass taxidermist eyes to make the buck's eyes

Because I hunt alone I have to rely on the camera's self timer if I want to do a hunter setup or photograph a buck I've killed, as in this case. With a little practice such photos are easy to take.

look fresh. They slip in like a human's contact lenses and can make a buck look like it did moments after it was killed. Also, take pains to keep the tongue in the buck's mouth and the mouth closed. If the mouth will not stay closed by itself, you can force it shut by inserting a small nail through the bottom of a buck's jaw and into its palate. If I kill a buck just before dark and want to photograph it in daylight, I gut it out, clean the hair to remove any blood, and lay the carcass on pallets overnight. Then, the next day the buck can be photographed after the glass eyes are inserted. Whatever you do, don't hang a buck by its antlers if you want to photograph it later. The weight of its body will cause the neck to stretch and the photos will not be realistic.

chapter 15

TOMORROW

Trudging through snow on a cold November dawn is not something that excites most people. But such a setting brings back vivid memories of deer hunting with my dad. I'll never forget my mom shaking me from a sound sleep to say, "Charlie, dad is getting ready to go deer hunting. Are you going with him?" Even at the age of seven I was eager to tag along at my dad's heels as he pursued the wily whitetail. Of course I was a liability to him, but it never stopped him from taking me.

Stopping for breakfast at the small local diner was another part of the hunt that sticks in my mind as though it was yesterday. In the predawn darkness the excitement surged within me as I stared at the red clad hunters devouring their breakfast before the day's hunt. If it was opening day they'd talk of bucks they'd seen or heard about. If it was later in the season the talk was about where they were going or who got lucky.

The experience of being beside my dad on watch in a deer woods was a thrill, though my patience was far shorter than his. More than once I cost him a shot at a whitetail because I moved too much. It frustrated him to no end, but he kept on taking me with him. Then there was the slate gray day in November of 1955, when I was next to him as he killed a beautiful buck. Though the three pointer was no trophy, I was as proud as a strutting peacock. I don't know who was more excited about it, he or I. It was pretty heady stuff for an eight-year-old.

No doubt many would cringe at taking such a young boy into a deer woods, especially in a part of America where hunting pressure is high. But we were farm folks and Dad believed in teaching his only son the ways of the woods early. He took me along until I was old enough to pull my own trigger. By the time my first opening day rolled around I knew what deer sign to look for and how to hunt deer. Those years of tagging along paid off that first year when I killed a nice seven point that field dressed 175 pounds. Since that first opening day I've never been skunked and much of my success is due to a man who thought it was important for his son to hunt.

Dad instilled in me more than just how to handle a gun. To him the hunt was also an appreciation of nature. The sound of chickadees chirping away while feeding in the hemlocks was special to him. Also, the experience of trailing a buck up one ridge and down another was something he enjoyed. To him killing a buck took a back seat to the feeling and excitement of just being in the woods, and he made sure I knew it as well. As I look back on it now, I not only see a man and his boy sneaking through the woods but also a teacher and a student. Dad built within me the foundation for my love of nature and deer hunting.

Sadly, I see much of this teaching/learning experience concerning hunting missing today. When I was growing up in the 1950s and 1960s America's thoughts toward hunting were much different than today. For one thing more people lived in rural areas back then and when people live close to nature, they tend to better understand its workings. As a result hunting was

Our kids are our future. From the time he was old enough to walk I've shared the woods with my son, Aaron.

more acceptable. Kids in my area were brought up to understand that whitetails were a crop, such as potatoes or corn, and had to be harvested if nature was to stay in balance. But somewhere this ideology slipped from the sportsman's grasp.

In 1993 the second annual governor's symposium on North America's hunting heritage reported that between 1955 and 1980 the percentage of the U.S. population over twelve years of age that hunted hovered between 9 and 11 percent. However, the percentage of hunters over sixteen years of age has steadily dropped, from 10 percent in 1975 to 7.5 percent in 1991. Currently there are approximately twelve million deer hunters in America and this number is projected to drop to about ten million by the turn of the century. Now, with fewer hunters in the field, people involved in the hunting scene are asking themselves, "Why the decline?" No doubt there are many reasons for the decline in hunting but four big ones are loss of hunting habitat, anti-hunter activity, lack of interest, and low recruitment.

These four points are perhaps the biggest reasons why youngsters are not becoming involved in sport hunting. Traditionally teens were taught to hunt by their fathers or other family members. But as America moved from an agrarian, or rural, society to urban surroundings this began to change. Today, with a more mobile society, the urban father often loses interest in hunting and in turn fails to teach his kids as dad and granddad taught him.

Statistics over the last ten years have shown that fathers are spending fewer and fewer quality hours with their kids. Also, the pressures put on parents who are trying to survive the urban grind simply leaves them with little free time. Consequently, unless the hunting tradition is firmly embedded in their souls, the hassles of driving to the country and trying to find a place to hunt cause parents to lose interest in hunting.

Much of hunting's success has come from the baby boom generation (those born in the late 1940s and early 1950s). Unfortunately one of the realities of hunting is that only a small percentage of hunters hunt after reaching fifty years of age. So, in the next few years there will be many hunters exiting the sport.

So, with fewer and fewer fathers taking the time to introduce their kids to hunting, who will teach them? The logical answer would seem to be sportsmen's groups. Though this is now beginning to happen, years of ground were lost. During the last fifteen years many youngsters throughout America were subtly being introduced to the idea that hunting was something ugly and not to be done. For the most part this idea has been perpetuated through the media. What baby boomer will ever forget the so-called documentary on primetime television titled "Guns of Autumn." It was not only highly emotional, but also influential to people uninformed about hunting. Unfortunately this anti-hunting bias continues unabated.

There is no guarantee this scene will always exist. The right to hunt is being threatened from many sides.

A few years ago while doing research for a magazine article, I learned much about the hunting/nonhunting pulse of America. The most startling thing was that about 80 percent of Americans do not hunt and know little about hunting. What they know comes from what they read, see, and are taught. At the same time the remaining 20 percent is split down the middle between hunters and anti-hunters. With these figures in mind it's easy to see how people, youngsters in particular, can be misinformed regarding hunting.

As a former public school board member here in New York State, it's easy for me to see how the anti-hunting bias penetrates the classroom. From the time a youngster starts public school at age five to graduation at eighteen, he has spent more than 17,000 hours in a classroom. During this time he has learned a myriad of things from painting by the numbers to calculus. For the most part the curriculum is excellent and by graduation students have learned much more than their parents did. It is also easy to see how students, taught mostly by nonhunting public school teachers, can be misled about hunting, fishing, and trapping in their general science and environmental courses.

John Dewey has been referred to in some circles as the "father of modern education in America." His influence on public education is enormous. One of his philosophies was that the thinking of a nation could be changed by indoctrinating those that teach the masses. It's almost like the anti-hunting leaders are following Dewey's lead because they are strongly influencing the teachers of tomorrow. Teachers graduating from college today tend to be more opinionated against guns and sport hunting than in the past. For those teachers with strong anti-hunting views, public school systems afford them a golden opportunity to instill their view in their students. Unlike sportsmens groups who must vie for time to address students, teachers have a captive audience for much of the day.

In our school district many teachers hunt and fish. Of those who don't, only a few could be classified as anti-hunting. However, the teachers who are nonhunters must deal with the subject the same way they would with anything else they are not knowledgeable about; they go to the resources available to them. It's these resource materials that often deal hunting a heavy blow. At our local level, the anti-hunting movies and videos available to teachers outnumber the hunting information nearly three to one.

It is here that hunting, fishing, and trapping suffer because the anti-hunting literature has had more going for it. For one thing the anti-hunting literature has tended to be more professionally done, though this is changing. Also, much of it tends to grossly misinform the urban-bred teachers with nonhunting upbringings. For the most part teachers I've been associated with make an honest attempt to tell both sides of an issue as

If the anti-hunters have their way, this scene could be eliminated in America. America's hunting tradition runs deep but it's only as strong as the next generation.

fairly as possible. But with so much anti-hunting literature available, their ideas concerning hunting often change.

Across this land wildlife organizations that were once pro-hunting are starting to drift toward the anti-hunting side of the ledger. For several summers I taught nature photography for one of the largest conservation organizations in the world. If I revealed its name, most hunters would recognize it immediately as an organization begun by hunters. Each year I was asked for a brief biographical sketch of myself for its handbook. The only thing the organization would not print in my bio was that I was a field editor for *Deer And Deer Hunting* magazine. After the second deletion I confronted the group and was told they didn't print it because it was too controversial. Certainly this in itself doesn't make the organization anti-hunting. However, my observations while teaching convinced me they were moving in that direction. Some of the things I gleaned from this teaching experience were sad. Why? Because they often misled people as to the role hunting has played in America's conservation movement. This happened mostly by ignoring the hunting issue altogether or sidestepping it.

The fact that this organization and other large conservation groups, who influence millions, don't give hunting its rightful place concerns me as I look to the future. The part the organizers of the Boone and Crockett Club and Ducks Unlimited played in bringing the wildlife populations of America back to their

October 15, 1993. This was my greatest thrill in the deer woods. After years of tagging along with me, my son killed his first deer with a bow and arrow. It is a joy to see the hunting tradition passed on to the next generation.

present levels seems to be conveniently ignored by many conservation groups. In 1900 various forces had reduced the whitetail's population to about 500,000. Through sportsmen's efforts, today's whitetail population hovers around 19 million whitetails in the United States. This turnaround didn't happen with smoke and mirrors. No, it took blood, sweat, and big money by the sportsmen of America to create this conservation miracle.

As an outdoor communicator I have the opportunity to address a wide range of groups during the course of a year. Usually the seminars not dealing with hunting revolve around my nature photography. Even at these programs I share with the audience that because of my hunting experiences I became a nature photographer. Through hundreds of programs over the last fifteen years I've been asked every imaginable question about hunting. By far the most frequently asked question, whether from an elementary school assembly or a flower club gathering is, "How can you photograph something so beautiful and also hunt and kill wild animals?"

Though most would view such a question as a program killer, I look forward to it. I enjoy telling people the positive side of hunting, especially if the group is made up of children. The adults may have voting power but these young minds hold the future. I share with them the history of hunting and how hunters brought back the wildlife populations we have today through self imposed management practices. I try to make them aware that stewardship and hunting go hand in hand. Part of the message is that if we as humans are to be responsible stewards of the resources God has entrusted to us, we must manage the wildlife as a renewable resource. And hunting is the only sensible management tool.

I always try to wrap up any seminar by stressing ethics. I view this as the catalyst in hunting's future. In my opinion the deer hunter's one great challenge in the next century is not how to kill a trophy buck but rather in proving he deserves to be in the field. It is important that we show the 80 percent who don't hunt that we are not slobs, poachers, or bloodthirsty mongers. Whether the hunter is a farmer, teacher, banker, factory worker, or corporate executive, the message he conveys must be one of integrity. Hunters should be ever mindful of game and trespass laws, if hunting is to see the light of day in the next century.

If hunters want to see deer hunting remain a recreational pastime and management tool, we'll have to do a better job of teaching the uninformed the hows and whys of the sport. No longer is deer hunting just the experience of purchasing a license, knowing how to shoot a gun, and searching for the elusive buck. It's all these and more--much more. To be a successful and responsible deer hunter requires not only woodsmanship but also a keen understanding of the politics and ethics of the sport.

During the past few years I've thought long and hard about the ethical side of hunting. Often I've thought, "How do we convey this message to young hunters and keep the sport of hunting healthy?" My conclusion is that it has to be demonstrated by actions and leadership. Just as my dad did with me, I introduced my son to hunting. As soon as Aaron was old enough to understand, we began discussing rubs, scrapes, sign interpretation, and the ethics of deer hunting. Our experience has been a blessing for both of us and in the fall of 1993 we reached another milestone when Aaron killed his first whitetail with a bow and arrow. My life as a hunter has truly been a special journey.

But what about those youngsters who don't have a dad who hunts? Who will teach them tomorrow, the sportsmen of America or the uninformed public? Edie Martin, a sportsmen's activist and outdoor columnist from Needham, Massachusetts, wrote, "Hunting's going to be referred to in the past tense unless we get sportsmen off their rearends, working to save their sports!" These are powerful words from a lady. Certainly we can ill afford to allow nonhunting educators in the public sector to teach our kids about hunting. So, who will teach them? The answer is us, you and me. And the time to start is not tomorrow, next week, or next deer season, it's now.

If we're to compete with anti-hunting's methods, sportsmen will have to commit themselves to doing things in a "high tech"

Three generations of white-tailed deer hunters: my son, my dad, and me.

way. Making contributions to pro-hunting groups such as the NRA, Wildlife Legislative Fund of America, and the Izaak Walton League will be as important as having a place to hunt.

As I reflect back on my life I think of the many blessings the sport of hunting has brought my way. It's only by the grace of God that I've come from being a farm kid to having one of the greatest jobs on earth. To me deer hunting is more than fancy equipment and mastering the latest strategies. It is a time-honored tradition, passed on from generation to generation. It's the experience of being in a tree stand on a crisp autumn morning. It's the joy of just being there.

Like most dads I have some pretty special dreams for my son Aaron. I've always wanted him to be able to experience the outdoors as I have. I want him to be able to chase bighorn sheep above timberline in the Rockies and watch Canada geese lift off a cattail marsh as I have. I want him to witness the sight of a white-tailed buck crashing through the brush in front of him. I also want him to realize that the shooting of a whitetail is not an evil thing but rather a part of life, stewardship, and the balance of nature. And lastly, I want him to realize that if he gets skunked he hasn't lost but rather has experienced the most important thing in deer hunting and that's the privilege of just being a participant. But unless sport hunting remains a part of our heritage, these dreams may never be realized and that deeply concerns me.

Some people have said hunting's future is "a crapshoot at best." I like to think our chances of saving the sport of hunting are better than that. The sport has changed greatly since I began deer hunting in the 1960s. While some of the changes have been bad, most have been good. And if we heed Edie Martin's words, then hunting and deer hunting in particular has a strong future. After all, we owe our kids the opportunity to hunt as we have and experience all that nature has to offer. That's what hunting is all about. Happy hunting.

Charles Alsheimer's Ultimate Deer Hunting Seminar

Each year Charles Alsheimer presents numerous fund-raising seminars across the country. This is a hard-hitting program dealing with a host of topics that are of interest to whitetail hunters across America, including: scouting, sign interpretation, scrape hunting, hunting whitetails with decoys, finding wounded deer, ethics and hunting's future - the most important subject, and many more.

". . . your presentation was terrific! Many in attendance stated that your program was the most professional in-depth seminar they had ever heard on the whitetail."

Corky N. Newcomb, organizer
New England Deer Hunting Show & Seminar
Manchester, New Hampshire

". . . thank you for the excellent deer hunting seminar. It was by far the best hunting program that has ever been to the Kane area."

Randy Durante, organizer
Kane Rotary Club
Kane, Pennsylvania

"A tip of the hat goes to Charlie Alsheimer. His deer hunting seminar and multi-media was outstanding. He truly knows the great outdoors and teaches all how to appreciate what God has given us."

Patrick P. Domico, marketing executive
The Progress Newspapers
Clearfield, Pennsylvania

For more information on how your group can raise funds hosting one of Charles Alsheimer's seminars, contact:

Charles Alsheimer
4730 Route 70A
Bath, NY 14810
(607)566-2781

SUGGESTED READINGS

Adams, Haas, Madson, Schuh, Rue. *The Outdoor Life Deer Hunters Encyclopedia.* New York. Outdoor Life Books, 1985. 788 pp.

Alsheimer, Charles J. and Watkins, Larry C. *A Guide to Adirondack Deer Hunting.* New York. Beaver Creek Press, 1987. 215 pp.

Bauer, Erwin A. *Erwin Bauer's Deer in Their World.* New York. Outdoor Life Books and Stackpole Books, 1983. 243 pp.

Bauer, Erwin A. and Peggy. *Whitetails - Behavior, Ecology, Conservation.* Minnesota. Voyageur Press, 1993. 155 pp.

Benoit, Larry. *How to Bag the Biggest Buck of Your Life.* Vermont. Whitetail Press, 1974. 158 pp.

Biggs, Mike. *Amazing Whitetails.* Texas. T.P.W., Inc., 1994. 191 pp.

Brothers, Al and Ray, Murphy E., Jr. *Producing Quality Whitetails.* Texas. Wildlife Services, 1975. 246 pp.

Etling, Kathy. *Hunting Superbucks.* Connecticut. Outdoor Life Books and Grolier Book Clubs, 1989. 445 pp.

Fratzke, Bob. *Taking Trophy Whitetails.* Wisconsin. Target Communications, 1983. 124 pp.

Fitz, Grancel. *How to Measure and Score Big Game Trophies.* New York. David McKay Co., Inc., 1977. 130 pp.

Halls, Lowell K. (ed.). *White-tailed Deer.* Pennsylvania. Stackpole Books, 1984. 864 pp.

Hofacker, Al. (ed.). *Deer and Deer Hunting.* Wisconsin. Krause Publications, 1993. 207 pp.

Horner, Kent. *Art and Science of Whitetail Hunting.* Pennsylvania. Stackpole Books, 1986. 190 pp.

Koller, Lawrence R. *Shots At Whitetails.* New York. Knopf, 1975. 359 pp.

Kroll, James C. *Producing and Harvesting White-tailed Deer.* Texas. Institute for White-tailed Deer Management and Research, 1992. 590 pp.

Miller, Greg. *Aggressive Whitetail Hunting.* Wisconsin. Krause Publications, 1995. 208 pp.

Morris, David. *Hunting Trophy Whitetails.* Montana. Venture Press, 1992. 483 pp.

Ozoga, John J. *Whitetail Country.* Wisconsin. Willow Creek Press, 1988. 146 pp.

Ozoga, John J. *Whitetail Autumn.* Wisconsin. Willow Creek Press, 1994. 160 pp.

Rue, Leonard Lee III. *The Deer of North America.* Connecticut. Outdoor Life Books, 1989. 544 pp.

Rue, Leonard Lee III. *The World of the White-tailed Deer.* New York. Lippincott, 1962. 137 pp.

Rue, Leonard Lee III. *Whitetails: Answers to All Your Questions.* Pennsylvania. Stackpole Books, 1991. 275 pp.

Smith, Richard P. *Deer Hunting.* Pennsylvania. Stackpole Books, 1978. 256 pp.

Storm, Tom. *Decoying Whitetails.* Montana. Tom Storm, 1991. 203 pp.

Trout, John, Jr. *Hunting Farmland Bucks.* Indiana. Midwest Hunting Productions, 1993. 228 pp.

Van Dyke, Theodore S. *The Still Hunter.* New York. Macmillan, 1882. 389 pp.

Wegner, Robert. *Deer and Deer Hunting: the Serious Hunter's Guide.* Pennsylvania. Stackpole Books, 1984. 316 pp.

Wegner, Robert. *Deer and Deer Hunting: Book #2.* Pennsylvania. Stackpole Books, 1987. 380 pp.

Wegner, Robert. *Deer and Deer Hunting: Book #3.* Pennsylvania. Stackpole Books, 1990. 350 pp.

Wegner, Robert. *Wegner's Bibliography on Deer and Deer Hunting.* Wisconsin. St. Hubert's Press, 1993. 330 pp.

Weishuhn, Larry. *Hunting Mature Bucks.* Texas. Krause Publications, 1995. 220 pp.

Weiss, John. *Advanced Deer Hunting.* Pennsylvania. Outdoor Life Books and Stackpole Books, 1987. 330 pp.

Wensel, Gene. *Hunting Rutting Whitetails.* Montana. Professional Impressions, 1982. 192 pp.

Wooters, John. *Hunting Trophy Deer.* New York. Winchester Press, 1977. 251 pp.

INDEX